The
SANDWICH
Generation's Guide
to Eldercare

The SANDWICH Generation's Guide to Eldercare

Kimberly McCrone Wickert, MRC, CRC

Danielle Schultz Dresden, MEd, CRC

Phillip D. Rumrill, Jr., PhD

demosHEALTH

NEW YORK

Visit our website at www.demoshealth.com

ISBN: 978-1-936303-43-4
e-book ISBN: 978-1-61705-142-5

Acquisitions Editor: Julia Pastore
Compositor: S4Carlisle Publishing Services

Medical information provided by Demos Health, in the absence of a visit with a health care professional, must be considered as an educational service only. This book is not designed to replace a physician's independent judgment about the appropriateness or risks of a procedure or therapy for a given patient. Our purpose is to provide you with information that will help you make your own health care decisions.

The information and opinions provided here are believed to be accurate and sound, based on the best judgment available to the authors, editors, and publisher, but readers who fail to consult appropriate health authorities assume the risk of injuries. The publisher is not responsible for errors or omissions. The editors and publisher welcome any reader to report to the publisher any discrepancies or inaccuracies noticed.

Library of Congress Cataloging-in-Publication Data

Wickert, Kimberly McCrone.
  The sandwich generation's guide to eldercare / Kimberly McCrone Wickert, MRC, CRC, Danielle Schultz Dresden, MEd, CRC, Phillip D. Rumrill, Jr. PhD.
      pages cm
  Includes index.
  ISBN 978-1-936303-43-4 — ISBN 1-936303-43-4 1. Aging parents—Care. 2. Adult children of aging parents. 3. Caregivers. 4. Sandwich generation. I. Dresden, Danielle Schultz. II. Rumrill, Phillip D. III. Title.
   HQ1063.6.W53 2013
   305.26—dc23
                              2013027231

Special discounts on bulk quantities of Demos Health books are available to corporations, professional associations, pharmaceutical companies, health care organizations, and other qualifying groups. For details, please contact:

Special Sales Department
Demos Medical Publishing, LLC
11 West 42nd Street, 15th Floor
New York, NY 10036
Phone: 800-532-8663 or 212-683-0072
Fax: 212-941-7842
E-mail: specialsales@demosmedpub.com

Printed in the United States of America by Gasch Printing.
13 14 15 16 17 / 5 4 3 2

Contents

Preface

With the ever-aging Baby Boomer generation consisting of more than 77 million Americans and the populace of the United States becoming older thanks to life-prolonging medical advances, more families than ever before face the challenge of providing care and support to multiple generations at the same time. Many people find themselves "sandwiched" among three and even four generations of their loved ones, and the needs of their children, parents, and grandparents can be difficult and even overwhelming to meet. Today, one out of every eight Americans between the ages of 40 and 60 is raising a child or children while caring for elderly parents or grandparents, according to Pew Research Center.

How do families navigate the complicated and costly process of planning for their children's futures, saving for their retirement, and providing the care and support that their elderly loved ones need? How do they know when it is time to make a change in housing or health care on behalf of an aging parent or grandparent? What are the legal, financial, emotional, and practical implications of eldercare decisions for the rest of the family? How can families, including blended families, minimize and/or manage the conflict and tension that often accompanies eldercare decisions? What are the best ways to help the elderly maintain their independence, dignity, and comfort even as they require more help with activities of daily living and decision making than they did in their younger years? What if the elder is gay, lesbian, bisexual, or transgender? What resources exist to help those "sandwiched" between generations to provide effective and responsive eldercare for their families?

The Sandwich Generation's Guide to Eldercare was written to answer these questions. In addition to our extensive experience in the rehabilitation and health care fields, the three authors of this book have all gone through the eldercare process with our own loved ones. We have flavored this book with our own eldercare experiences and the insights of other members of the Sandwich generation who have gone through this process with their loved ones. Intended for people who are providing eldercare for their loved ones while raising families of their own, health care professionals in geriatrics and long-term care, rehabilitation professionals, social workers, counselors and psychologists, health care and assisted living administrators, benefits planning specialists, and college and university students in related disciplines, this book serves as a guide to eldercare developed by those who have done it. We hope that the lessons we have learned through our own personal and professional experiences will help you and your loved ones in your efforts to help them age in comfort and with dignity.

Kimberly McCrone Wickert
Danielle Schultz Dresden
Phillip D. Rumrill, Jr.

Acknowledgments

We would like to express our sincere gratitude to the people who made this book possible and successful. First and foremost, we recognize our parents and grandparents whose needs for eldercare and experiences with aging in contemporary America prompted us to write this book: Judy McCrone, Henry McCrone, Fay Wickert, Stewart "Papa" Schultz, Beverly Rumrill, and Harry Rumrill. Watching these ordinary heroes age while attempting to maintain their independence and dignity made us realize that countless families face the same daily challenges of caring for aging loved ones that our families have tried to navigate. It is our hope that some of what we have learned about eldercare in our own families, coupled with our professional experience in the human services field, will be useful to others in the Sandwich generation who are responsible for the care, comfort, and well-being of their own heroes.

And speaking of heroes and loved ones, we know that we could not have completed this book without the love, support, and forbearance of our beloved spouses. Scott Wickert, Jason Dresden, and Amy Rumrill lent their (usually) constructive criticism as proofreaders, editors, technical consultants, sounding boards, coaches, therapists, and cheerleaders throughout this project. Often, they provided direct and clear feedback about the content of our book, the time we devoted to writing it, our performance as spouses and parents vis à vis our writing activities, and a variety of other subjects without even being asked! Only the most devoted spouses and partners would be so free and generous with their perspectives. In all seriousness, we know how fortunate we are to be sharing our lives with our best friends, our steadfast partners, and our true loves. Scott, Jason, and Amy—we thank you from the bottoms of our hearts.

This book focuses on the generations that came before us, namely, our parents and grandparents, but we want to acknowledge the generation that will succeed us as the inspiration for everything we do. The Oak Ridge Boys had it right: "Thank God for Kids." We thank God for ours: Jake Wickert, Delaney Wickert, Ben Martin, Jenae Martin,

Blake Dresden, Connor Pittman, Nathan Rumrill, Doug Rumrill, Stuart Rumrill, Cassidy Pittman, and Chad Pittman. Jake, Delaney, Ben, Jenae, Blake, Connor, Nathan, Doug, Stuart, Cassidy, and Chad—thank you for constantly reminding us of the wonder of youth, for the smiles and laughter that keep us young, for the chores you occasionally do without being asked, for not rolling your eyes too often or too obviously when we tell you stories about our own childhoods, and for giving our lives purpose and meaning that can only be found by raising children. And, if our deep gratitude and profound pride in you are not acknowledgment enough, you may be interested in knowing that we will use the royalties from this book to increase your allowance!

For their editorial and clerical assistance, we thank Mr. Jesse Wray and Ms. Samantha Haynie of Kent State University. Special thanks go to Dr. Mary Dellman-Jenkins, Attorney Margaret Kreiner, Mr. Jim Krosky, Attorney Wade W. Smith, Jr., Attorney Kelly Willis, and Mr. Karl Zalar whose professional expertise and insights made invaluable contributions to this book.

Last, but certainly not least, we extend our heartfelt appreciation to Julia Pastore and the editorial staff at Demos Health for the opportunity to write and publish this book. We look forward to many more collaborative endeavors in the years to come.

ONE

You Are Not Alone: The Graying of America and the Role of the Sandwich Generation in Providing Eldercare

The face of America has been changing, or graying, more accurately. The United States now boasts a senior population that is larger than at any other time in the country's history, and the proportion of elderly people in the American populace is likely to increase for the next several decades. According to a report from the U.S. Census Bureau, in 1980 there were 720,000 people aged 90 and older in the United States. In 2010, there were 1.9 million people aged 90 and older; by 2050, the ranks of people 90 and older may reach 9 million. Increased life expectancies are one reason for the projected growth in our senior population, but the large population of Americans who are currently in middle age is the main reason for the expected increase in elderly people over the next two or three decades. Termed "Baby Boomers," these people are identified by birthdates between 1946 and 1964 and number approximately 77 million. As Baby Boomers continue to age with longer life expectancies than their parents had, the number of Americans over the age of 65 is expected to double by 2030. So, too, can we expect a commensurate increase in the number of senior citizens who require assistance in performing activities of daily living.

With longer life expectancies comes an increased reliance on health care and pharmaceutical interventions. Many physical and sensory disabilities increase in incidence as a function of age, including vision and hearing loss, arthritis, orthopedic impairments, diabetes, and heart and lung disease. There is also a significant increase in the rate of dementia as the population ages; more than 7 million Americans are currently living with this disease. Dementia is caused by changes to brain cells that can affect memory, reasoning, language skills, physical functioning, personality, and interpersonal interactions. Although this progressive condition can be treated to some extent, there is no cure, and people with dementia require increasing care and treatment for the remainder of their lives.

We continue to see the ratio of workers to retirees fall as our population ages, which has a significant impact on our nation's overall economic productivity. According to the Population Resource Center, in 1970 there were almost four workers for every Social Security beneficiary. Today there are 3.3 workers for every beneficiary and that ratio is expected to decline to 2.2 to 1 by the year 2030. According to the Administration on Aging, the major sources of income for older persons in 2008 were Social Security (reported by 87% of older persons), income from assets (reported by 54%), private pensions (28%), government employee pensions (14%), and earnings (25%). These numbers add up to more than 100 percent because most people over the age of 65 have more than one source of income. The median income of older persons in 2009 was $25,877 for males and $15,282 for females. Households containing families headed by persons aged 65 years or older reported a median income in 2009 of $43,702. These income levels enable many elderly people to cover their living expenses as long as they remain healthy and can live independently, but many seniors find the cost of eldercare prohibitively expensive once their health begins to decline. Life gets more expensive as a person's age advances, and elderly people usually find their income staying the same or decreasing over time, which increases the number of senior citizens who find it difficult to support themselves financially.

Medical and pharmacological advances have extended life expectancies and improved quality of life for many elderly Americans, but the rising costs of health care continue to have a major impact on our economy in general and on elderly people and their families in particular. Over the next 20 to 40 years, there will be more elderly Americans than at any other point in history, and current trends suggest that the elderly will be more reliant on financial support from their families than ever before. These realities are chiefly responsible for the common projection that the Sandwich generation—people, usually in middle age, who are raising their children and/or grandchildren while caring for their parents and/or grandparents—will be the first generation of Americans to be worse off during retirement than their parents.

Experts have blamed the poor general economy brought on by the Great Recession, the decline of the housing market, and exorbitant health care costs for much of the financial anxiety elderly people and their families feel as they plan for the future. Many elderly people believe they have significant equity in their homes as part of their long-term financial holdings, but, when they seek to draw on that equity to downsize their homes or to provide income for living expenses and health care, they often find their homes worth less than expected. This often requires the elderly person to seek financial assistance from family members in the Sandwich generation and/or to move in with their children or grandchildren to defray expenses.

The challenge of maintaining a home becomes even more complicated for an elderly person when family members, friends, and/or paid assistance must be enlisted to help the person perform household tasks that he or she formerly performed independently. Many people choose at this time to consider smaller homes with lower utility costs, less maintenance, and greater accessibility. Apartments, retirement communities, and assisted living facilities are considered as housing options at this time, depending on the person's health status and needs for assistance. Other people opt to make renovations to their existing homes to make them more comfortable and accessible. A 2011 *USA Today* article indicated that 62% of National Association of Home Builders members were working on housing renovations related to aging. One in five builders were adding at least one bedroom to the first floor of their customers' homes. Even so, many elderly people simply cannot afford the ever-rising costs of housing, home repairs and maintenance, property taxes, and long-term care, which forces them to move in with family members.

An encouraging trend for senior citizens can be seen in the increased lobbying power and attention they are receiving from politicians, government agencies, businesses, and health care providers. This growing population is enjoying strength in numbers, and the voting and purchasing leverage of older people has placed the needs and concerns of elderly Americans at the forefront of our national policy agenda. The American Association of Retired Persons (AARP) regularly weighs in with considerable influence on public debates regarding Social Security, health insurance coverage, prescription medications, and other important issues. Retailers, restaurants, movie producers, hotels, airlines, and automobile manufacturers directly target senior citizens in their marketing and advertising efforts.

Certainly, America's older people can look to many celebrity role models who have maintained active and productive lives after traditional retirement age. Senators Edward Kennedy, Bob Dole, and John McCain made some of their most important contributions to our society after the age of 65. Performing artists such as the Rolling Stones, the Beach Boys, Neil Diamond, Bob Dylan, Willie Nelson, Paul McCartney, and Merle Haggard have continued to record and perform music during their twilight years. Actors Clint Eastwood, Betty White, Shirley MacClaine, Jane Fonda, Morgan Freeman, Jack Nicholson, and William Shatner have all recreated their careers as they have aged. Talk show hosts Joan Rivers and Regis Philbin and newsmen Mike Wallace and Andy Rooney could be seen on television into their 70s and 80s. Sportscasters Vin Scully, John Madden, and Al Michaels have continued to call games. Football coaches Eddie Robinson and Bobby Bowden roamed the sidelines into their 80s. Numerous books in recent years have been written by Joseph Wambaugh, Larry McMurtry, Cormack McCarthy, Kurt Vonnegut, and Gore Vidal—all of whom were over the age of 75 when their most recent books were published.

Although politicians and celebrities may enjoy continuing to work well after the traditional retirement age, many ordinary Americans are doing so out of financial necessity. Even after retiring from full-time work, many seniors secure part-time positions to offset health care costs, pay for housing and living expenses, and/or provide financial support to adult children or other family members. This semi-retirement phenomenon often requires families to consider employment issues facing their elderly loved ones as they plan and implement needed care.

~

A Personal Story: Adaline and Her Family

Adaline is a 76-year-old woman who has lived in the Great Lakes Region of the Midwest her entire life. She graduated from high school in 1954, was married in 1958, and had her first child, a daughter named Rhonda, in 1961. She had her second child, Steve, in 1965. She worked as a shipping clerk and clerical support person until she retired at the age of 62. Adaline, along with her older sister, cared for their mother in her home until she passed away at the age of 100. Until last year, Adaline had lived in the same town all her life. When she was younger, Adaline loved to go out and dance with her friends, and she enjoyed entertaining friends and family in her home. She was known as an excellent cook, and she was often prevailed upon to bring her delectable cheesecake to potluck dinners and other social events. Adaline has always had a soft spot in her heart for animals, especially dogs and cats, and she is still known to have a "green thumb" when it comes to indoor plants and outdoor gardening.

Following her retirement from her shipping/clerical work with the same company for more than 25 years, Adaline worked at several part-time jobs, including one as a cafeteria worker in an elementary school. She also worked as a home health aide working with individuals with developmental disabilities. She quit working altogether in her late 60s.

Adaline considers herself an independent woman. She and her husband, David, divorced in 1967. Since then she lived alone and depended upon her older sister, who is now 78, to help her out. She also had several friends who would visit her often and assist her with errands. Her son Steve lives 90 miles away. Her daughter Rhonda lives in California. Over the past few years, Adaline had gradually exhibited increasing signs of dementia as evidenced by her short-term memory loss; inability to make rational decisions; difficulties performing such tasks as overseeing her bank account, taking her medication, and caring for her home; and her increasing habit of misplacing personal items. She developed some effective coping mechanisms, and, although she was aware of many of her limitations, she continually expressed a desire to remain independent.

Adaline's friends and family noticed her decline in functional abilities and were concerned about her well-being living alone. One indication of her diminishing ability to live independently came when she was still driving and got lost on her way to her son's home, a destination she had driven to dozens of times over the previous 10 years. She began to report unusual incidents with her automobile such as someone reportedly backing into her when she opened her car door at a gas station and the passenger side mirror suddenly "falling off" the car. She also ran a stop sign while driving in front of her son. A family friend reported that she found Adaline wandering in the local cemetery, unable to find her car after visiting her mother's grave. Adaline reluctantly gave up driving following these incidents at the insistence of her children, Steve and Rhonda. She then relied upon her sister and neighbors to take her shopping and run other errands.

Recognizing her diminishing ability to live independently and manage her own affairs, Steve and Rhonda sought assistance for their mom from a variety of local agencies. Although she did not like the idea, Adaline had an assessment conducted by the Area Agency on Aging in her county. The case worker provided resources to Adaline and her children to begin to develop a plan to ensure that she remained in a safe environment given her ongoing and increasing functional deficits.

At the time of her assessment, Adaline was being treated by several different physicians including a primary care physician, an endocrinologist for diabetes, a gynecologist, and a cardiologist. As her psychological symptoms increased, it became more challenging to effectively manage all of her medical care as well as medications given the number of providers treating her. At one point her family realized she had taken her medication outside of her prescribed dosage and had ill effects as a result. Her children spoke to her about seeing a geriatric specialist to undergo a complete medical evaluation and receive a diagnosis as to why she was exhibiting these increasing symptoms. Another objective for seeing a geriatric specialist was to have one provider oversee all her medical care including medication management and treatment.

Reluctantly, and only after strenuous urging by Steve and Rhonda, Adaline consented to the appointment with the geriatric specialist. Neurological testing, including a magnetic resonance imaging (MRI) scan, revealed a diagnosis of vascular dementia. The geriatric specialist told Adaline, Steve, and Rhonda in no uncertain terms that she was no longer able to be alone in her home. Adaline wished to remain in her home, so Steve and Rhonda sought the assistance of a home health agency. For several months, Adaline received assistance at home from the agency, albeit reluctantly, while Steve began to oversee her financial and medical affairs. Because Adaline was no longer able to independently manage her medication regimen, this responsibility was assumed by the home health agency on a daily basis. Steve traveled 90 miles to Adaline's home once each week to check on her and prepare her medication, and her older sister, Carol, visited her at least once per day. Her friends and neighbors continued regular contact with Adaline, often taking her to visit their homes or to attend community events.

As Adaline's symptoms increased, it became increasingly difficult for Steve to tend to her from a distance while meeting the needs of his own family, and Steve and Rhonda decided, after one year of in-home care, that it was time to move Adaline closer to one of them. The financial cost of in-home care, which by this time she needed on a 24-hour basis, was certainly a consideration, but even more importantly Steve and Rhonda believed that Adaline needed more local support than her neighbors and her also-aging sister could provide. Steve lived in the same state, so it was decided that Adaline would move to Steve's community.

Steve arranged for Adaline to move into an assisted living facility less than a mile from his home. Steve and Rhonda had been exploring this as an option for several months and met with the assisted living facility on multiple occasions to plan the transition process. Adaline's level of dementia did not allow her to participate much in the decision to move her to the assisted living facility in Steve's community, but she definitely did not favor the idea at first. Steve, Rhonda, and Adaline's sister Carol consulted with Adaline's geriatric specialist throughout the transition into Adaline's new home. The initial plan was that she would remain in the assisted living apartment for at least the winter so that Steve and his family would be able to see her on a daily basis to provide emotional support and oversee her medical care. Part of the transition plan was that Steve would spend the first several nights with her in her new apartment to make her feel more comfortable. Carol and Rhonda, who visited from California for two weeks during Adaline's move, stayed with Adaline during the day, so for the first several days she was with family at all times in her new surroundings. Adaline and her family met the staff and other residents of the assisted living facility, which made everyone more comfortable with Adaline's move to her new home.

Adaline transitioned as well as could be expected into the assisted living facility. Being closer to his mom and seeing her every day, Steve and his family began to see the severity of her dementia on a daily basis. Although the initial plan was a temporary one in theory, Adaline's family quickly realized that going back to her home and living alone was no longer an option. A year later, Adaline continues to live in her assisted living apartment and keeps busy every day with activities including going out to restaurants, attending symphony concerts, shopping, and participating in the many events that occur at the assisted living facility.

Although Adaline's family has had to adjust to seeing her dementia take a stronger hold on her every day, an adjustment process Steve and his wife describe as very much like grieving, they are satisfied knowing she is in a safe place near their home, which makes it possible for them to see her on a daily basis. She has also developed a very close relationship with her grandchildren, who enjoy visiting her and including her in their school and sports activities.

~

THE ROLE OF THE SANDWICH GENERATION IN ELDERCARE

The Sandwich generation refers to adults, usually between the ages of 40 and 60 (although they can be younger or older), who are raising children while at the same time caring for parents or grandparents. The Sandwich generation does not discriminate—it includes people of both genders, representing all religions and every racial and ethnic group. Membership in the Sandwich generation is not restricted based on health, socioeconomic, or marital status. The Pew Research Center reveals one out of every eight Americans between the ages of 40 and 60 is currently in the middle of the sandwich of care and responsibility, supporting minor children while caring for an elderly parent or grandparent at home. Also according to the Pew Research Center, an additional 7 to 10 million people between the ages of 40 and 60 are raising children while providing support to an elderly loved one from a distance.

And members of the Sandwich generation know that life does not stop or even slow down when an elderly loved one needs care. Most members of the Sandwich generation work full-time, and they must attend to their own health and retirement planning while caring for their children and parents. Not surprisingly, the bulk of responsibility for care and support for children and elderly family members falls upon women. Thirdage.com says that approximately 70 percent of primary Sandwich generation caregivers are female.

Balancing parental and eldercare responsibilities while maintaining employment is a major concern for members of the Sandwich generation. Fifty-two percent of women and 34 percent of men between the ages of 40 and 60 have experienced interruptions in their work days due to family eldercare issues, according to the Metropolitan Life Mature Market Institute. The Boston College Sloan and Family Research Network reported that workers are less productive when they are worried about the care and support of an elderly family member.

The National Alliance for Caregiving reported that 33 percent of large employers nationwide have eldercare programs to support employees who must care for their aging loved ones. Eighty-one percent of large and small employers allow workers to take time off for eldercare responsibilities without jeopardizing their jobs. While it is financially difficult for many to give up working to care for a child or aging parent, the financial impacts also affect the employer. According to a survey by the National Alliance for Caregiving and the MetLife Foundation, workers caring for elderly relatives cost companies in the United States approximately $34 billion annually in lost productivity, absenteeism, and replacement costs. Caregivers may be able to access services such as legal, financial, and mental health counseling to assist in eldercare and childcare needs through an organization's employee assistance program. Flexible spending accounts also allow an employee to place money in an account that is not subject to payroll taxes to cover dependent care costs. The Family and Medical Leave Act of 1993 allows employees of businesses or agencies with 50 or more workers to take unpaid time off to attend to their own health concerns or the health concerns of family members.

A word to Sandwich generation caregivers regarding the Patient Protection and Affordable Care Act, also known as Obamacare—if your own health insurance coverage is provided by your employer, it is important to remember that employers are only required to provide health insurance coverage for employees who work 30 hours per week or more. Many employers are worried that they will not be able to afford health insurance coverage for all of their 30-hour per-week employees, so they may seek to decrease the number of employees who work that many hours while increasing the number of part-time employees as a means of decreasing their health insurance costs. So, if you are currently working 30 hours per week or more and receive health insurance benefits from your employer, it is important to know that reducing your hours below 30 per week may jeopardize your benefits. And if you are thinking about changing jobs, it is important to know that employers might be doing more part-time hiring than full-time hiring, with part-time hiring carrying no requirements to provide health insurance coverage.

Modern communication technology has also helped the Sandwich generation in its efforts to balance work and family responsibilities. Many employers allow their employees to job share or work from home part or all of the time, which affords workers the flexibility to attend to important family responsibilities while doing their jobs. The Internet, email, webinars, Skype, cellular technology, and other electronic forms of communication have allowed those in the Sandwich generation to stay in touch with their parents and children while working from home. Those same technologies enable people to perform some eldercare tasks from long distance.

Many members of the Sandwich generation feel unprepared for the eldercare responsibilities that are often unexpectedly placed upon them by changes in their aging family members' health status. They may lack the financial means to support their loved ones in the manner they would like to. Their homes may not be large enough to accommodate additional people, or they may not be accessible given their parents' or grandparents' changing physical abilities. And of course, new members of the Sandwich generation have focused their caregiving efforts on raising their children—they have no experience providing eldercare services.

It is natural to fear the unknown when taking on eldercare responsibilities for the first time, but many experts have suggested that the skills involved in raising children provide excellent preparation for eldercare. In many ways, parenting amounts to individualized case management of all aspects of a child's life, and individualized case management is the essence of effective eldercare. As the authors of this book reflect on our own eldercare experiences, we recall drawing heavily upon the things we learned as parents to help us in managing the care and support of our elderly loved ones. Organizational skills we developed in choosing and monitoring medical care for our children helped us in making health care decisions on behalf of our parents and grandparents. Financial planning skills we utilized in following household budgets and saving money for college when our children were young helped us to manage our elderly loved ones' financial affairs. Childproofing strategies to ensure that our children were safe in our homes were generalized to some extent to the safety measures we had to implement when our parents and grandparents moved in with us. So, even though parenting is quite different from eldercare in terms of the developmental levels of the people being cared for and the specific content of advocacy and planning that are required, members of the Sandwich generation who assume eldercare responsibilities may already have many of the skills required to protect the safety, well-being, and dignity of their elderly parents and grandparents.

~

A Personal Story: Steve, a Member of the Sandwich Generation

Steve is a 47-year-old husband, father of two children, and son of Adaline. He was raised in a small Midwestern town until he went away to college in 1986. He obtained a bachelor's degree and secured a job as a marketing representative four hours away from where his mother lived. Steve married Kate in 1990. While he was working full time, Steve began working on his master's degree in Business Administration, which he completed in 1997. Also in 1997, Steve was promoted within his company and relocated to a community 90 miles from where his mother lived at the time.

Steve and Kate had their first child, a son, in 2000 and their second, a daughter, in 2003. When their children were very young, Steve and Kate began to notice Adaline repeating the same stories over and over, and she would ask the same question several times within one telephone conversation. Her memory, judgment, thought processing, and behavior became major concerns.

Two years ago, Steve began working with Kate, his aunt, and his sister to develop a plan for Adaline's care. Soon after he noticed the beginnings of Adaline's psychological decline, he encouraged her to establish a will, durable power of attorney, medical power of attorney, and living will. Steve lived 90 miles away from his mother at that time, and he was concerned that he would not be able to provide care for her from that distance. Adaline's memory was deteriorating steadily, and there were a few occasions when Steve suspected that local home repair contractors had been taking advantage of his mother. Adaline's older sister, Carol, Steve's aunt, was helping Adaline as much as she could, but her advancing age made it difficult for her to meet Adaline's increasing needs, especially as Adaline's dementia progressed. The family decided to consult a geriatric specialist.

Prior to consulting the geriatric specialist, Steve and his family thought that Adaline might have Alzheimer's disease because many of her symptoms were similar to those associated with that condition. As mentioned in Adaline's story, her diagnosis of vascular dementia was revealed during her geriatric assessment. Steve and his family realized that this diagnosis was serious and that Adaline needed a number of changes in her daily care. The in-home care was a temporary solution until a more permanent plan was developed. Steve and Kate realized that it would be increasingly difficult over time to coordinate Adaline's care, oversee her finances, and guide her daily activities from a distance of 90 miles.

Before long, Steve and Kate began to look for assisted living facilities closer to their own home. They discussed moving Adaline into their home, but they both worked full time and in-home care or geriatric daycare would need to be provided during the work day. Given their work schedules and responsibilities, the costs of in-home care and geriatric day care, and the demands of caring for two young children, they opted to bring Adaline to an assisted living facility within walking distance of their home. This would allow Steve and his family to see her daily, plus he would not have to make the 180 mile round trip to check on her every week during the winter months in the snow belt region of the country.

Steve and Kate determined that making Adaline's move during December would allow the family flexibility during the holidays to spend more time with her during her transition. They developed a schedule so that Adaline would be with someone in the family at all times during her first few days in the assisted living facility. Steve's sister, Rhonda, who lives in California, visited for the first two weeks of Adaline's relocation to provide support.

Rhonda continues to visit periodically, but Steve and Kate are chiefly responsible for Adaline's care.

Steve and Kate had gone through the process of choosing pre-schools and day care facilities for their children several years earlier, and they found themselves employing some similar strategies in deciding upon an assisted living facility for Adaline. They toured the facility several times before making the final decision, recognized the need to help Adaline adjust to her new surroundings by staying with her for the first few days, and dropped in unannounced at the facility to see staff members interacting with residents during the height of daily activities. Steve and Kate wanted their children to feel comfortable at the assisted living facility and in Adaline's apartment, so they brought games and craft boxes to her room as well as stocking her refrigerator with the children's favorite snacks and beverages. Steve found his children to be an effective distraction when Adaline would focus on her declining abilities or her desire to go home. Being with the children brought Adaline great joy and comfort, and the children enjoyed having their grandmother so close by.

Steve and Kate presented the move to Adaline as a temporary one for the winter to allow everyone to be closer together and avoid the treacherous road conditions he had encountered on many occasions when he had to drive such a long distance to see her each week. Adaline did not want to relocate 90 miles away from the town she had lived in her entire life, but she did not want to be a burden to her son. She agreed to move to the assisted living facility in Steve's community to make things easier for Steve and Kate. Thinking of her relocation as (ostensibly) temporary allowed a smooth transition for Adaline, and it gave Steve a chance to gradually come to terms with his mother's declining health. Although Steve knew that her functional abilities had diminished, he was optimistic at first that having 24-hour medical care, medication management, and proper nutrition would improve Adaline's health and, possibly, allow her to return to her home one day if provided with needed assistance. Although Adaline's move to the assisted living facility turned out to be permanent, it gave Steve some initial comfort to consider this move a trial relocation.

Immediately after Adaline moved into the assisted living facility, Steve began to fully understand the impact of her memory loss and general psychological decline. Following her first night in her new apartment, she woke up disoriented, not knowing where she was and unable to recall that she had moved into the apartment the previous day. Steve and his family were happy that they would be able to spend more time with Adaline, but it quickly became evident that her symptoms would not improve and that she would need to stay in the assisted living facility on an ongoing basis.

Steve continues to find it difficult to balance his responsibilities for his mother's care with his responsibilities as a husband, father, and professional worker. He mourns the memory he has of his mom as a strong, competent, and stubbornly independent woman. Prior to the onset of her dementia, Adaline always provided care and nurturing for Steve, Kate, Steve's sister Rhonda, and Steve's children, but the roles are reversed now, and these people who were the beneficiaries of Adaline's care and nurturing are now being called upon by the situation to be the caregivers and nurturers. (This is precisely the situation in which millions of Americans in the Sandwich generation find themselves.)

Although Steve realizes that Adaline is now in a place that allows her to flourish with daily activities, social opportunities, and caring staff members, he struggles with feelings of guilt because he placed his mother in an assisted living facility even though she had insisted in the past that she wanted to remain in her home for the rest of her life. Steve continues to maintain and pay taxes on her home, which is 90 miles away from the assisted living facility, but he realizes that he will one day need to liquidate her assets to pay for her stay in the assisted living facility. Steve and Kate worry that Adaline will not have enough money to keep her in the assisted living facility on a long-term basis, which would leave the financial responsibility for Adaline's care and housing to them.

Steve tries to focus on the positive aspects of having his mother in a safe environment where he can support and monitor her on a regular basis. He is thankful that his children are getting to know their grandmother in a much closer way thanks to the regular contact they have with Adaline. Adaline appears more relaxed and happier than she has been in years. She is comfortable in her new surroundings, has made many friends, and enjoys many of the activities offered within the assisted living community.

Steve communicates with his aunt (Adaline's sister) and his sister Rhonda on a regular basis. He gets along well with both of them, and they support one another in making decisions about Adaline's care. Both his aunt and his sister appreciate Steve's willingness to take the lead in arranging Adaline's care and overseeing her affairs.

~

YOU ARE NOT ALONE

As the Baby Boomer generation continues to age and Americans in general can expect longer lives than ever before, the need for elder-care is likely to increase dramatically over the next several decades. Already busy with child-rearing responsibilities, career considerations, and their own retirement planning, middle-aged Americans will increasingly be called upon to arrange, provide, and/or monitor care for their aging parents and grandparents.

This book was written for you if, like millions of people in the United States, you find yourself sandwiched between generations of people who need and depend on you. We in the Sandwich generation are often willing to provide support for any family members who need it, but we may exceed our financial, physical, and psychological capacities in the process if we are not careful about eldercare. The already-complicated middle years of adulthood can become overwhelming when an elderly family member requires assistance in managing his or her housing, finances, transportation, nutrition, and health care. But, friends, you need not despair—there is strength in numbers, and you are not in this alone!

Approximately 12 percent of people such as us, between the ages of 40 and 60, are raising children while caring for elderly loved ones, and that percentage is likely to increase throughout our lifetimes. With the increased responsibility placed upon the Sandwich generation have come many strategies and resources that can assist you and your family in caring for multiple generations at the same time. The following chapters are filled with practical information designed to help you do the most important thing you will ever do—care for the people you love.

"Where do we start?" "Who can help us?" "What kind of help do we need?" "How do we know that the resources we find are reliable?" These are the questions that members of the Sandwich generation ask when they first realize that their parents or grandparents need help with eldercare. The daunting and emotional process of gathering information and determining what services and facilities are best suited for your loved one can be overwhelming, to say the least. There is no reason to expect that you should be prepared from the outset to help your elderly loved one make decisions about his or her care—you haven't done this before. Remember, too, that this is a time of realization that your loved one is moving toward the final stages of his or her life. There are many complicated and important decisions to make, and this is a stressful time for you, your family, and your elderly loved one. You will need help finding answers to all of the questions you have, but help is available.

TWO

Is it Time?:
Determining When
It's Time to Take
Over the Care of Your
Loved One

- When and how to intervene
- Recognize common "red flags"
- Use an assessment checklist
- Deal with the adjustment process

A fall, a sudden change in health status, or a change in the health status of a caregiver or spouse may thrust you into the caregiving role of an aging parent or loved one without warning or advance planning. The below steps will help you in a crisis situation:

- If the emergency situation is due to a medical issue of your loved one, first and foremost, make sure he or she is medically stable through use of hospital care, primary care physician services, respite care, home health care, or any other means available.
- Gather as many legal, medical, or financial documents as possible. Having your loved one's insurance and Medicare/Medicaid information is crucial during emergency medical treatment. (See Chapter 3 for detailed information on important legal, financial, and health care documents.)
- Locate and gather any medication your loved one takes to assist. This could prove to be of invaluable assistance to medical personnel in the treatment process.
- Create a list of contact names and numbers to notify those who need to be involved in the situation.

- Tap into your resources and support system, including family and friends, for assistance.
- Once your loved one is medically stable and in a safe environment, proceed to Chapter 3 for help making a long-term plan.

EMERGENCY PLANNING

Do

- Ensure that you as the caregiver have delegated your responsibilities such as childcare, carpool, and after-school activities.
- Notify your employer if your work will be impacted.
- Have copies of important documents such as insurance card, prescription card, power of attorney, bank information, and so forth, available.
- Identify who is the decision maker or power of attorney if one is not already designated.
- Reassure your children that everything is going to be OK if you are suddenly absent to provide emergency planning, and so on.
- Ensure you have the ability to communicate on an ongoing basis with devices such as a cell phone with an extra power cord or charger.

Don't

- Panic. Try to remain calm and assess the situation to identify what is needed to move forward.
- Jump to conclusions. Get the facts in order to make an informed decision.
- Make decisions solely based on guilt, anger, or a negative past experience.
- Forget to take care of yourself during this crisis situation.

If it is not an emergency situation, determining the appropriate time to take over or make a change in the care of your elderly loved one is a difficult decision but a necessary one. This decision is fraught with anxiety, potential conflict, and, for many people, mixed feelings. On one hand, you want your parent or grandparent to be comfortable in whatever surrounding he or she chooses for the rest of his or her life. On the other, you have to be concerned about the safety of your elderly loved one as well as the well-being of other family members, including yourself.

It goes without saying that the "right" time to take over the care of an elderly loved one varies from person to person and situation to situation. The physical and emotional proximity of an elderly loved one to the caregiver has a significant impact on the caregiver's ability to determine when to step in. Having regular, close contact with the elderly person makes it easier to identify changes in the person's health status and ability to live independently, whereas infrequent contact or communication makes it difficult to assess the person's needs.

If you live far away, ask other family members or friends if they've noticed any changes in your loved one. In the example of Steve and Adaline, who lived 90 miles apart, the initial signs of Adaline's psychological decline were less apparent to Steve than they were to Adaline's sister, who saw her on a daily basis. Another option is to enlist the services of an agency or organization specializing in geriatrics to obtain an objective and complete picture of an elderly loved one's status. These include Area Agencies on Aging, social workers, and geriatric case managers and can be found at places such as Eldercare Locator, a service of the National Association of Area Agencies on Aging at 800-677-1116, or www.eldercare.gov. Or you may wish to obtain an expert medical opinion via a geriatric examination with a physician or other geriatric medical specialist. Additional resources can be found in the Eldercare Experts and Eldercare Resources A–Z sections of this book.

GERIATRIC CARE MANAGERS (GCM)

A geriatric care manager assesses an elder's ability to live independently in a home environment, develops an appropriate care plan for services and equipment, and organizes needed home care services. The GCM also continues to review and monitor the plan to coordinate ongoing services and may include financial planning as part of their larger care management offering. GCMs may also be known as eldercare managers, case managers, and service or care coordinators. GCMs hold certification from the National Academy of Certified Geriatric Care Managers (NAPGCM), often in addition to another certification or licensure such as rehabilitation counselor, social worker, or registered nurse.

GERIATRIC SPECIALISTS

Focusing on the unique needs of the elderly, geriatric specialists often treat individuals 75 years of age and older and are familiar not only with the medical diagnoses most common to the elderly, but also the social and emotional issues that are common when working with this population. Geriatric specialists may be board certified in Geriatrics or Family Practice with additional training to obtain a Certificate of Added Qualifications in Geriatric Medicine (CAQGM.)

When assessing and treating an elderly patient, the geriatric specialist will consider: immobility, instability, cognitive/intellectual function, hearing, vision, and incontinence. In addition to these areas, a geriatric specialist will consider social and emotional status, independence, and other items such as psychological status in an effort to promote good health as well as quality of life.

Geriatric specialists also provide support to family members and caregivers who may be experiencing stress and seeking additional information related to this role. These practitioners often have a team of professionals to assist them in providing a holistic approach to the treatment of an elderly patient and his or her caregiver such as nurses; occupational, physical, and speech therapists; dietitians; pharmacists; and social workers.

A family doctor can certainly treat an elderly individual, but physicians specializing in geriatrics focus on the diagnoses and diseases common to this population. People of advanced age have bodies that are physiologically different from those who are younger, so a geriatric specialist might be best suited to meet your elderly loved one's age-related needs. For example, having a slight fever or urinary tract infection may have minimal impact on a middle-aged healthy adult's overall health and functioning, but a fever or infection in an elderly person can have a much greater impact on his or her health and safety.

Medication management and usage in older adults can also be much different than that of other populations. Specialists in geriatrics are schooled in the use of medication in the elderly population. Some medications may be inappropriate for use in older adults, and a geriatric specialist is aware of what medications to avoid. Additionally, geriatric specialists are aware of how medications can be used in tandem to enhance desired effects for diseases such as Alzheimer's and dementia. Elderly individuals are prone to taking multiple medications, which is known as polypharmacy. This may be a combination of herbal, over-the-counter, and prescription medications.

The geriatric specialist may also be able to oversee the medical care of the elderly loved one. In some cases, if the elderly person sees multiple physicians, the geriatric specialist can monitor all of the care and ensure that communication is occurring among all parties involved in your loved one's medical treatment. The holistic team approach can also support the caregiver in providing counseling and support to deal with the stress of caring for a loved one.

When searching for a geriatric specialist, you may want to ask prospective physicians the following questions:

- Are you willing to be interviewed by me or my loved one to allow us to choose our provider?
- How many years of experience do you have treating the geriatric population?
- Who provides coverage for your practice when you are on vacation?
- How long does it take to get an appointment to see you?
- Are same-day appointments available?
- What is the average wait time in your office?
- With what hospital or health care system are you affiliated?
- Are you affiliated with any assisted living or skilled nursing facilities?
- Do you complete "rounds" at any assisted living or skilled nursing facilities?
- Do you maintain paper or electronic files?
- Do you take questions by email?
- Do you accept my elderly loved one's insurance coverage?
- What certifications do you hold?
- What are your office hours? Do you have evening or weekend hours?
- How does your office handle emergency or after-hours calls?
- Do you offer lab services, and, if so, what tests are available onsite?
- What is the make-up of your team of geriatric specialists, such as nurses, social workers, dietitians, and physical, occupational, and speech therapists,?
- How would you characterize your communication style or bedside manner?

Other issues to consider in selecting a geriatric specialist include proximity to your elderly loved one's home, the availability of parking at the office or facility, whether the specialist offers house calls, and references from other patients and/or other doctors.

In Adaline's case, the geriatric examination provided a comprehensive review of Adaline's physical, psychological, and environmental history, including her present level of functioning and capability. It also provided important information for developing a plan of care to ensure that Adaline was in a safe and appropriate environment with effective medical and pharmaceutical treatment.

SIGNS IT MAY BE TIME TO STEP IN

Although there is no all-inclusive list of "red flags," there are many indicators that a change may be needed in your elderly loved one's care. These include:

A change in mental or physical health status. These may include a change in mood or personality or cognitive deterioration such as being unable to perform simple activities like making a phone call. A change in physical health status may include a newly diagnosed disease or condition, a sudden change in physical capacity due to a fall or other injury, or more subtle changes like a sudden loss of weight.

Decreased functional abilities, including memory loss, disorientation, misplacing and losing personal items. Carol first noticed Adaline's memory loss when Adaline struggled to remember important dates such as her children's and grandchildren's birthdays, holidays and vacations, and family anniversaries. When an elderly loved one becomes disoriented in places that are familiar to him or her, this is a sign that it is time to examine other care options that would not place the person in such situations unless he or she is accompanied.

Decreased physical capabilities. These may include difficulty walking or falling while attempting to walk. Other examples of decreased physical capacities include inability to perform daily hygiene tasks unassisted or difficulty changing positions from sitting to standing or bending down to pick up an object on the floor.

Difficulty performing everyday activities such as grooming, dressing, driving, housekeeping, and cooking. Difficulties with driving and cooking pose serious safety risks and must be addressed immediately.

Inability to manage medications and nutritional intake. Running out of medication too early or still having medication in the bottle at the time of renewal are indications that medication is not being taken as prescribed. AARP reports that 25% of elderly people admit to skipping doses of medication or cutting them in half. A 2005 survey of 17,685 seniors conducted by the Kaiser Family Foundation, the Commonwealth Fund, and Tufts-New England Medical Center found that more than one third of senior citizens report noncompliance with medication schedules. Medication noncompliance is, of course, especially problematic among elderly people who have cognitive impairments stemming from Alzheimer's disease or dementia.

Adaline was not taking her medication at prescribed dosage levels, and she would often take expired medication. An inspection of her refrigerator revealed food that was not properly wrapped and many food items that were well beyond their expiration dates. Adaline would also store perishable food items such as meat and dairy products in kitchen cupboards and on countertops.

Difficulty making or keeping track of financial decisions. Significant changes in a loved one's ability to manage his or her finances are usually red flags that a change in care is needed. Adaline had several thousand dollars that she could not account for over a few months' time. She also had mail and bills scattered all over her house in a disorganized fashion. At one point, Adaline's sister Carol realized that Adaline had not made a mortgage payment in 3 months. This inability makes the person vulnerable to unscrupulous people who may seek to take advantage of him or her. Adaline was involved in some dealings with building contractors that seemed questionable, and Steve had to intervene.

New compensating behaviors. During the early stages of Adaline's dementia, her keen sense of humor and interpersonal skills allowed her to conceal many of her emerging limitations from family and friends. For example, Adaline would sometimes remember in the middle of a story that she had already told the story to the same people on several occasions. Rather than drawing attention to her diminishing memory, she would jokingly tell the listeners that she was repeating the story on purpose to see if they were paying attention. She would also compensate for her memory loss by adding details to the story that she had not shared in previous versions.

Below is a checklist of questions designed to help you decide the right time to make a change in your loved one's care. We call it the "Is It Time? Checklist." The more "yes" answers you give, the higher the likelihood that you or someone else needs to step in.

IS IT TIME? CHECKLIST

☐ Do you find yourself worrying about the safety of your loved one?

☐ Do you call more frequently to "check in" on your loved one?

☐ Have you been stopping by your loved one's residence more frequently?

☐ Do you find yourself completing more chores for your loved one, such as mowing the lawn or house cleaning?

☐ Has your loved one's housekeeping or hygiene become a concern, such as lack of bathing or wearing dirty clothes?

☐ Has your loved one had accidents or "close calls" while driving?

☐ Have you noticed safety and security issues in his or her home, such as placing mail or newspapers on the stovetop, obstacles on the floor that may be a fall risk, or forgetting to lock the doors?

☐ Have you noticed old or expired food left out or in the refrigerator?

☐ Has your loved one experienced a recent weight change?

☐ Is your loved one susceptible to marketing or telephone scams?

☐ Does your loved one frequently misplace items such as a purse, keys, cell phone, or remote?

☐ Have you taken over the responsibility of scheduling and/or attending medical appointments?

☐ Do you take your loved one for simple errands such as grocery shopping?

☐ Do you have conversations with other family members or close friends regarding your concerns for your loved one's safety?

☐ Does your loved one repeat stories or ask the same questions repeatedly?

☐ Do you assist your loved one with getting the mail, paying bills on time, and balancing the checkbook? Did this begin due to late payments or creditors contacting your loved one?

☐ Has your loved one had a large increase in unexplained expenditures?

☐ Has your loved one complained of falling or sustained unexplained bruises or other injuries?

☐ Has your loved one complained of getting lost while driving?

☐ Has your loved one started a story and then forgotten the subject or been unable to finish?

☐ Have your loved one's prescriptions run out earlier than the refill date or are there still pills left in the bottle at the time of refill?

☐ Do you (the caregiver) feel overwhelmed with the responsibility of caring for your loved one?

☐ Have you (the caregiver) been experiencing symptoms of anxiety or other stress-related symptoms such as hives or high blood pressure?

☐ Have you (the caregiver) delayed dental and medical appointments or procedures because you are too busy caring for your loved one or others?

If you answered "yes" to even a few of these questions, consider discussing these issues with your elderly loved one. Elderly individuals need to feel included in the decisions that affect them regardless of their functional levels. Honesty is, indeed, true love, and it is important to be honest and forthright with the elderly family member at all times. Discuss your concerns or the signs that suggest it is time to take over the care and support of a loved one with the elderly person himself or herself. Listen to what they have to say. Communicating is very important as you make the decision to step in or make a change in your loved one's care.

Many of us are uncomfortable having the conversation with our elderly parent or loved one about his or her inability to continue to care for him- or herself unassisted. Attempting to be respectful yet realistic may present challenges to the potential caregiver. While it may seem like overkill, scripting the conversation and practicing with a friend or another family member is an option. Be honest but compassionate in your presentation of information and provide specific examples of why you are concerned about your loved one. Have this conversation in a setting that is comfortable for your loved one as well as you.

Try to conclude the conversation with a few action steps you can agree on (speaking with a physician, making accommodations in the home, etc.) or further fact finding (specific resources available in the community). Be sure to follow up on them.

~

A Personal Story: Joseph and Dani

Joseph grew up in Michigan in the 1940s and 1950s. As a boy, he enjoyed riding and caring for his horse, Lightning. Joseph experienced many medical setbacks in his life, beginning when he was only 18 years of age. Joseph joined the Army at 18 and was deemed totally disabled by the time he was 20. During boot camp, Joseph had a boil removed from his neck during a routine physical examination follow-up. While home on leave a few months later, he was watching a movie with some friends when he suddenly felt an excruciating pain in his left hip area. When he returned to his army base, he was diagnosed with osteomyelitis. It was determined that the core of the boil had traveled through his bloodstream and attached to his pelvic bone, which aggravated the osteomyelitis.

Joseph underwent more than 20 surgeries related to his osteomyelitis from age 19 until his late 20s. His left hip was fused, which resulted in his left leg being 2 inches shorter than his right leg. Joseph did not let his physical limitations deter him from leading a normal and productive life. He married and had three children, Anna, Dani, and Sean. He attended college and became an x-ray technician. He worked in hospitals throughout his career. Toward the end of his career, he acquired hepatitis C.

Several years after he retired, Joseph separated from his wife, left his lakeside home in Florida, and returned to the Midwest to be near his children, who were grown by this time. Shortly after moving back north, Joseph's psychological and medical health began to decline. He began forgetting things like where he was going on driving trips and the names of people he knew well. Joseph was hospitalized after complaining of chest pains and feeling disoriented. Now 65 years old, Joseph was diagnosed with transient ischemic attacks (TIAs, also known as mini-strokes). After his condition stabilized, he was released from the hospital. He moved in with Dani, his oldest daughter, to recuperate. Soon, Joseph felt strong enough to return to his home.

Over the next few months, Joseph's health declined quickly. He sustained more TIAs and was hospitalized again. Many more hospital visits came over the next few months. He needed more and more assistance as time went on. It was determined that he would move in with Dani and her family. Due to Joseph's weakened physical state and his memory problems, it was no longer safe for Joseph to drive. He reluctantly gave up his car keys, on the provision that if his health improved Dani would arrange a driving assessment for him at a local rehabilitation hospital.

Dani's home was an older home with the bathroom and bedrooms on the second floor. This made Joseph reliant on Dani and her husband for assistance up and down the stairs. After a few weeks, Dani and her husband realized that their home was not arranged in a way that was conducive to Joseph's increasing needs for accessibility and assistance. The couple then purchased a home that already had an "in-law" suite to accommodate Joseph and his needs.

The following year, Dani gave birth to twins and was now caring for her dad and her growing family while working a full-time job. (These circumstances placed her in the Sandwich generation.) Joseph was able to complete many of his own activities of daily living at first, but as time went on he needed more help with other things such as managing his medications, keeping track of his finances, and monitoring his health status and medical care. Dani took over dispensing Joseph's medications, handling his finances and scheduling all doctors' appointments.

One spring day, Dani went into her father's room to check on him as she did each morning. He was shaking slightly and seemed disoriented. Joseph said he did not sleep well the night before and was just tired. Dani helped him into the recliner in his room and turned on his television. She told him she needed to make a phone call and would be back to check on him in a little while. Moments later, Joseph walked past Dani, who was on the phone, and he was shaking and grabbing onto various household items to stabilize himself. Once he gained his balance, he went out the front door, seemingly in a hurry. Dani abruptly ended her call and followed Joseph outside, where she found him lying on the ground and bleeding. She called 911. An ambulance came and transported him to the hospital.

At the hospital, Joseph was diagnosed with dementia. Several doctors asked about his care at home. It was determined that he would go to a nursing/rehabilitation center prior to returning home. During his stay at the nursing/rehabilitation center, Joseph acquired pneumonia. This resulted in additional limitations including incontinence and difficulties in walking. Joseph returned to Dani's home with daily in-home health care. A problem soon became evident in that Joseph's dementia made it difficult for him to communicate his needs to his caregivers. He would frequently tell them that he did not need a shower, and he would sometimes not tell them in advance when he had to go to the bathroom. These tasks would then become Dani's responsibility in the evening when she returned home from work.

Joseph had received ongoing psychiatric treatment for depression and anxiety since he was injured in the military as a young man. Dani told Joseph's psychiatrist at Veterans Affairs that she was becoming more and more worried for his safety when home health care was not present. Joseph's behavior was becoming increasingly unusual, even bizarre at times. He decided to resume smoking after 30 years as a nonsmoker, and he became very adept at sneaking cigarettes and matches from visiting relatives and friends. He would also forget periodically that he was reliant on a walker, so when he would get out of bed in the middle of the night to smoke cigarettes, he would sometimes fall down and become alternatingly angry, disoriented, embarrassed, and sad. He would awaken Dani and her family at all hours of the night demanding his medication, which he forgot he had already taken during the day. Mealtimes were difficult propositions, as well; Joseph would often insist that he was not hungry even though he had not eaten since the last meal, or he would demand food immediately after a meal he did eat.

After Joseph had a severe bout with the flu, Dani was exhausted and emotionally drained from the daily toll of taking care of her children, working full time, and caring for her father. She contacted Joseph's psychiatrist at Veterans Affairs to discuss her concerns regarding Joseph's care and safety. Dani asked the doctor to provide indicators to the appropriate time to explore long-term care in a skilled nursing facility. She was struggling with the fact that she would probably not be able to meet her dad's needs in her home anymore. The doctor said, "You asked when the right time is—it's the right time now." The doctor went on to explain that, when the caregiver asks when is the right time to explore the next step in an elderly loved one's care, that is when it is time for the next step.

~

In the story of Joseph and Dani, Dani struggled with what many people who care for elderly loved ones do in knowing when to assume and/or change the care for that individual. She consulted with a professional who had been treating her father to help determine the next step, and she had to balance her father's need for care and his wishes to stay in her home with her own best interests and the best interests of her children.

With Joseph, the progression of his dementia provided Dani with the evidence that she needed to make a change in his housing and overall care situation. Dani reached the point where she could no longer accommodate Joseph's increasing limitations and still care for him safely in her home. His growing disorientation, unpredictable behavior, and inability to remember when he took his medicine or ate meals told Dani that something needed to be done to safeguard the well-being of all concerned. Dani became convinced that relocating Joseph to a skilled nursing facility was the right thing to do, the responsible thing to do, considering the interests of Joseph, Dani herself, and Dani's children.

In writing this book, we interviewed dozens of members of the Sandwich generation regarding their eldercare experiences. One man who had recently been sandwiched between parental responsibilities and eldercare for his mother discussed a situation that occurred in our local community where, when a young adult man who was developmentally disabled was left unattended and became seriously injured. His mother had to answer charges of neglect. The man we interviewed commented that this unfortunate story reminded him that his responsibility to care for his children and his mother had legal ramifications as well as moral ones. He concluded that his hesitancy to place his mother in an assisted living facility, mostly because she did not want to relocate, could have jeopardized his mother's health and safety. He would have held himself morally responsible for any harm that came to his mother while she was living alone, and he speculated that he might have been subject to criminal liability as well. It is easy for parents to keep in mind that they are legally responsible for the care of their children, but sometimes members of the Sandwich generation need to be reminded that taking on the care of an elderly loved one brings legal responsibilities as well.

EMOTIONAL ISSUES OF CAREGIVING

You may experience a variety of emotions as you consider taking a more active role in your loved one's care. Every person will respond differently to the emotions that he or she experiences during the caregiving process. Responses may also hinge on the present as well as past relationship of the caregiver and elderly loved one. Emotions may range from relief to guilt or anger and everything in between. Looking at this as a transitional time may help everyone involved to work through this process more easily.

Role Reversal

In making the decision to take over or change the care of an elderly loved one, the phenomenon of role reversal often comes into play. Parents and grandparents are accustomed to caring for their children and grandchildren, not the other way around, and it is not uncommon for elderly people to resist overtures from younger generations to provide care and support. The issue of role reversal can also be a challenge for the adult child.

In the situation with Joseph and Dani, Joseph was the unquestioned patriarch of the family who provided for his wife and children despite the challenges he faced as a young man. He overcame many obstacles to work hard, be successful, and raise his children. Dani found it difficult to tell her father—this strong, proud, and self-reliant man who had always been the one to take care of her—that she needed to take care of him. Joseph's psychiatrist at Veterans Affairs told Dani that her discomfort in reversing the long-standing roles that Dani and Joseph occupied in their relationship was a normal feeling for a caregiver. This validated Dani's uneasiness about the decision she had to make, and it helped her to proceed with her dad's best interests at heart. She even discussed the matter with Joseph, who seemed to understand what she was saying for the first few minutes of the conversation but then changed the subject by asking her to make him a sandwich—even though he had just eaten a hearty breakfast.

To say that Adaline was not receptive to Steve's initial offer of care and assistance would be a vast understatement. This self-proclaimed strong, independent woman had to be convinced that she needed help because of her increasing limitations, which was a difficult proposition because she had become quite adept at minimizing and concealing those very limitations from those close to her. Steve also found it helpful to bring in an outside professional to help.

Communicating with your loved one is the key to dealing with role reversal. Even if your elderly loved one is unable to fully participate in the decision-making process, including him or her in conversations can make the role reversal process less taxing. Consider using the resources of a professional, such as a counselor, geriatrician, social worker, or clergy, to help as well.

Grief

When families first recognize the need for eldercare on behalf of a loved one, they often go through a process that is similar to the one described in Adaline's story. Watching the person you love lose his or her independence and ability to perform tasks that he or she once did without assistance, and often with a zest for life, is often a traumatic experience. Although your elderly loved one may still be physically present, many of his or her characteristics or abilities may have been lost, which places you into a grieving process for the person you once knew and loved. Grief and mourning are not to be avoided at this time—they are normal reactions to this often profound sense of loss that you and your elderly loved one experience as his or her health declines.

Elisabeth Kübler-Ross's Five Stages of Grief—denial, anger, bargaining, depression, and acceptance—provide a framework for understanding the sense of loss that you and your elderly loved one may be experiencing. Denial is the first phase of Elisabeth Kübler-Ross's Five Stages of Grief. Many families of loved ones become stuck in the denial phase. The remaining stages are anger, bargaining, depression, and acceptance. Some caregivers may find themselves moving from one stage to the next and back again based on the current functioning of the loved one, as well as the status of the oversight of the care of that person and their possessions.

Denial. During this first stage, a person is avoiding the loss he or she has experienced. Numbness may become an overwhelming and familiar feeling and some may question what once made sense in life. Not only is an individual in denial during this stage, he or she is often in shock as well. An individual may question his or her ability to continue to exist and identify simple ways to get through each day. Kübler-Ross states that denial is a pacing mechanism during the early stage of grief. She says that it is nature's way of only letting in what one can handle. Denial leads to the reality of the loss and eventually the start of the healing process. As one becomes stronger, denial begins to fade and feelings will surface.

Anger. Even though it is a necessary stage of the healing process, anger may seem endless when it first manifests itself. As one works through the feelings of anger, the anger begins to dissipate. Combined with many other emotions, anger can be all consuming, and it may be misdirected at the people who are closest to you, including the person in your family who requires care. Other targets of anger may include friends, doctors, oneself, and God. Some may question their religious beliefs during this time. Beneath the anger exists pain. Most people know more about suppressing anger than feeling it, but it is important to process feelings of anger with a trusted friend or loved one, or with a professional counselor if necessary. Anger is one of the least rational human responses to stress or grief, so trying to talk someone out of being angry is usually fruitless. Talking about the feelings that underlie the anger, and developing socially appropriate and safe strategies for expressing anger, are two of the best ways to work through this often painful stage of grief and mourning.

Bargaining. Bargaining is a usually internal process of attempting to restore the person's life to its status before he or she experienced the loss. When grieving the decline of an elderly loved one, people in the bargaining stage often ask "What if?" and "Why me?" or "Why my mom?" questions. It is also not uncommon during this stage to try to engage in activities that one used to do with the elderly person before his or her health declined. Perhaps you recall taking your dad back to a favorite fishing hole he took you to when you were a child, or taking your mom shopping at the mall she used to frequent. These attempts to go back in time are normal and may be enjoyable, although they can be frustrating if the elderly person cannot experience the event the way he or she remembers experiencing it in the past. Bargaining might also include casting decisions in a temporary context, such as inviting a parent to move in with one's family for a few days or a few weeks even when the person knows that his or her elderly loved one will have to relocate on a permanent basis.

Depression. After bargaining, it is not uncommon for some degree of depression to set in. Grief in this stage intensifies and may become overwhelming, and the mourner may feel that the sadness and hopelessness will last forever. Whereas bargaining focuses on the past and the way life used to be, depression focuses on the future and the loss that the person is experiencing in the here and now. Mourners need not have a history of depression to feel depressed over the decline of a loved one, and feeling depressed at this stage of adjustment does not necessarily mean that someone will be more susceptible to depression in the future.

Acceptance. Acceptance should not be confused with being "alright" or "OK" with what has happened. This stage is about accepting the reality that one has sustained a loss, and, in the case of an elderly loved one, it is usually the loss of that person's independence, capacity to live the life he or she loved, personality traits, and/or ability to communicate. Acceptance is about learning to live with what is a new reality in the life of your elderly loved one. The roles that people play in their families change during this time, and attention turns to helping the elderly person continue his or her life in the safest and most dignified way possible. So, too, do caregivers earn the right in the acceptance phase to move on with their own lives even as they are caring for their elderly family members.

For Steve, denial played a role in the slow, deliberate decision to take over his mother's care. He did not want his mother's life to change the way it was changing, and sometimes in the early stages it was easier for him to pretend that the changes were not happening. Adaline herself operated in the denial stage when she first began to decline—she developed elaborate strategies to hide her limitations from friends and family.

Denial continued to be a factor for Steve even after they transitioned his mother into an assisted living facility. For example, regarding his mother's home, he was hesitant to put it up for sale even though he knew she would never be able to live there again. He began bargaining, longing for the past when his mom was the nurturer and caregiver, not Steve. He then became angry that his mother was in this condition and also depressed and guilt-ridden that she was living in an assisted living facility. Adaline had insisted to both of her children that she wanted to stay in her home for her entire life, no matter what. Bargaining would manifest in the form of Steve putting Adaline's transition in a temporary perspective; although he knew this was a long-term solution, it was an effective coping strategy for him to put into place initially on a temporary basis. This can be a good coping mechanism for many families and elderly when taking over the care of a loved one.

During this time it's important to remember that your elderly loved one is adjusting to the changes in his or her life just as you and the rest of the family are, but he or she may be attempting to adjust to life changes at a time when his or her intellectual and emotional faculties are not what they once were. The decline in intellectual and emotional faculties can be scary for your loved one. Based on his or her cognitive abilities he or she may be aware of his or her decline and how it is impacting functional abilities and mental health status. Going through the stages of grief may also be part of this process as the caregiver and sometimes even the elderly loved one grieve for a time when the roles were more traditional in nature.

YOU'VE DECIDED IT'S TIME: TAKING THE NEXT STEP AND MAKING A PLAN

In the next chapter, we'll walk you through the process of making a plan. Whether you are fortunate enough to have the time to plan for your eldercare needs or if you are in the crisis-planning process for your loved one, planning is essential. We will identify a number of ways that you as the caregiver can create a practical plan for the legal, health care, and financial needs of your elderly loved one.

THREE

Making a Plan: Practical, Legal, Health Care, and Financial Essentials

- Create an eldercare plan
- Get important documents in order
- Ensure benefits
- Involve other family members
- Do's and don'ts

The last thing most of us want to do is spend our time planning for our decline and ultimately our demise. However, to ensure that your next of kin does not have to guess as to what you would want for your care as you age, or for your final arrangements, having a plan in place is critical. The same is true for your elderly loved one. If he or she has not already created an eldercare plan listing their preferences for care, then now is the time to do so.

The benefits of an eldercare plan are that it allows the elderly loved one to participate in identifying his or her needs and preferences when he or she is able to do so. The plan also avoids questions the caregiver may have about the loved one's preferences when the loved one may no longer be able to provide that information.

Knowing his or her preferences will not only help you as a caregiver in planning but may also assist in avoiding any disagreements among family members. At times, we operate based on information that is provided in partial fashion or based on how a situation may appear at a certain point in time. When the situation or factors change, such as a person's physical or psychological status as well as the demands of the individuals who are providing care, everyone may be thrown into unknown waters, experiencing stress and uncertainty as a result. This is especially true when there is an emergency or sudden crisis. Karl Zalar, a nursing home administrator, has seen the negative emotional and financial consequences to families who come to a crisis point due to a lack of planning. He recommends a comprehensive 5-year plan that is updated annually as the best antidote.

Creating an eldercare plan with the help of your loved one, siblings, and other family members, can help prevent rash decision making and disagreements. The plan may need to be amended as the situation changes but it will provide a baseline for revision and a useful tool for making the necessary adjustments.

If the elderly person is in a psychological and medical state where he or she can communicate and provide input, it is important to consider that person's preferences for eldercare. Although this is a subject that most people are reluctant to bring up with their parents or grandparents because it is uncomfortable and emotionally challenging, frank and open discussions about the family's capacity to care for an elderly loved one can help caregivers and care recipients alike when the time comes for a change in care. The plan allows your loved one to voice his or her opinions and preferences regarding long-term care planning. This will allow your loved one to be involved in the decision making and will also provide you with a guide if your loved one is one day unable to make his or her own decisions.

Use the Eldercare Planning Document on the following pages to help identify this important information in an effort to develop a plan that will allow you to incorporate their preferences. The eldercare plan should be signed by the loved one if possible and should be reviewed at least annually or when changes to the plan occur and provided to the family members who are involved in the caregiving process. It should be easily accessible to the primary caregiver and should be stored with the other important documents discussed in this chapter.

If your elderly loved one is not able to complete this worksheet, you and other family members can complete it on his or her behalf. Many assisted living and skilled nursing facilities ask questions about your loved one's preferences as part of the admissions process, so completing this worksheet can help you and your family communicate with other care providers.

ELDERCARE PLANNING DOCUMENT

Completed by: Date:

My family should assist me in my care when I: (Indicators that you may need additional assistance.)

_____

_____

_____

Individuals I would like to be involved in my long term care are:

Name	**Phone**	**Email**

Spouse/Significant Other:

_____   _____   _____

Siblings:

_____   _____   _____

Children:

_____   _____   _____

Friends:

_____   _____   _____

_____   _____   _____

_____   _____   _____

(continued)

ELDERCARE PLANNING DOCUMENT (*continued*)

Health Care Professionals:

_____   _____   _____

_____   _____   _____

_____   _____   _____

_____   _____   _____

_____   _____   _____

Pastor/Priest/Rabbi:

_____   _____   _____

Other:

_____   _____   _____

My Preference for Care/Treatment Is to Take Place in:
(Number these in the order you prefer)

_____My Home

_____Senior Residential Location

_____Assisted Living Facility

_____Skilled Nursing Facility

_____Other (Describe:_____)

(continued)

ELDERCARE PLANNING DOCUMENT (*continued*)

My Preference for Care Outside of My Home Is to Take Place at:

(List any medical facilities, assisted living facilities, or skilled nursing facilities you prefer to provide your care.)

_____

_____

_____

_____

Amenities That I Wish to Have With Me From My Home Are:
(Personal items examples may include favorite clothing, jewelry, bed, TV, lamp, chair, bedspread, pictures, mini fridge, phone, etc.)

_____

_____

_____

_____

Medication Information and Management
Physicians/Specialists That Provide Treatment to Me:

Name	Phone Number	Specialty
_____	_____	_____
_____	_____	_____
_____	_____	_____
_____	_____	_____

Prescription/Drug Name	Diagnosis	Dosage
_____	_____	_____
_____	_____	_____

(continued)

ELDERCARE PLANNING DOCUMENT (*continued*)

_____	_____	_____
_____	_____	_____
_____	_____	_____
_____	_____	_____
_____	_____	_____
_____	_____	_____
_____	_____	_____

Allergies or Sensitivities to Medications Include:

_____

Food Allergies/Sensitivities Include:

_____

Food Preferences Include:

_____

Financial Income and Asset Information

Monthly Income Source and Amount:

_____

Bank Name/Account/Amount:

_____

Bank Name/Account/Amount:

_____

401K/IRA/403B Information:

_____

(continued)

ELDERCARE PLANNING DOCUMENT (*continued*)

Pension Information:

_____

Life Insurance Carrier/Amount of Coverage:

_____

Health Care Insurance Coverage:

_____

Long Term Care Insurance Coverage:

_____

Transportation

Check all that apply.
- ☐ Vehicle I own/operate
- ☐ Vehicle I own/someone else drives
  - ☐ Friend/Family Member
- ☐ Local area transit
- ☐ Other (walk, bike, etc.)

Personal/Social Information

Social Interaction:
- ☐ I prefer to be socially active
- ☐ I am socially shy
- ☐ I prefer to interact in groups
- ☐ Groups make me anxious
- ☐ I prefer to interact one on one
- ☐ Other_____

My Daily Routines Are:

Morning Wake Up Time:
Breakfast time:
Breakfast preferences

- ☐ Eggs
- ☐ Toast/English muffin

(continued)

ELDERCARE PLANNING DOCUMENT (*continued*)

☐ Cereal
☐ Oatmeal
☐ Grits
☐ Malt O Meal/Cream of Wheat
☐ Waffles
☐ Pancakes
☐ Bacon
☐ Sausage
☐ Granola
☐ Protein or breakfast bar
☐ Breakfast sandwich
☐ Doughnuts
☐ Muffins
☐ Other _____

Activity:_____

Afternoon:

Lunch Time:

Lunch Preferences:

☐ Tuna fish sandwich
☐ Turkey sandwich
☐ Ham sandwich
☐ Soup
☐ Cheese and crackers
☐ Fruit
☐ Yogurt
☐ Salad with vegetables
☐ Salad with chicken
☐ Other _____

Afternoon Activities:

Dinner Time:

Dinner Preferences:

☐ Pasta with sauce (meatballs or sausage)
☐ Lasagna
☐ Macaroni and cheese

(continued)

ELDERCARE PLANNING DOCUMENT (*continued*)

☐ Grilled chicken
☐ Steak (What temperature do you prefer?)
☐ Soup (What kind do you prefer?)
☐ Frozen dinners (List several that you like.)
☐ Roast
☐ Ham
☐ Pork chops
☐ Hamburgers
☐ Hot dogs
☐ Casserole

Side Dishes You Prefer:

☐ Mashed potatoes and gravy
☐ Pasta
☐ White rice
☐ Brown rice
☐ Vegetables (Cooked or raw?)
☐ Salad (Dressing type?)
☐ Stuffing
☐ Macaroni and cheese
☐ French fries
☐ Fruit
☐ Cottage cheese
☐ Bread and butter
☐ Other _____

Snacks:

☐ Potato chips
☐ Yogurt
☐ Fruit
☐ Nuts (What kind?)
☐ Applesauce
☐ Cheese crackers
☐ Other: _____

Drinks:

☐ Coffee (regular or decaf)
☐ Water
☐ Tea
☐ Soda

(continued)

ELDERCARE PLANNING DOCUMENT (*continued*)

☐ Lemonade
☐ Juice (What type?)
☐ Other: _____

Evening Activities:

Other Activities:

Weekend activities I prefer are:

_____

Religious activities I prefer are:

_____

Work or tasks that I like to do are:

_____

My hobbies are:

_____

Sports and activities I like are:

_____

Music I like is:

_____

If I could have a pet in my home it would be:

_____

A good way to transition into a long term care facility for me is:

_____

Additional Information I would like to have considered in the event I am unable to share this at the time I require long term care:

_____

_____

_____

Signature   Date

_____   _____

GETTING IMPORTANT DOCUMENTS AND BENEFITS IN ORDER

Estate Planning

There are numerous reasons to make sure your loved one's estate is in order. Among them is peace of mind for both you and your loved one. It is also helpful to avoid potential disagreements among family members, while ensuring you are honoring your loved one's wishes when possible. Another reason is to make the transition process as smooth as possible for you as the caregiver.

Estate planning is critical for lesbian, gay, bisexual, transgender, and queer (LGBTQ) seniors and same-sex couples. Same-sex couples are not afforded the same rights as heterosexual couples, so it is important to create estate planning documents that clearly spell out how health care and financial matters will be handled. Laws vary state-by-state and a local lawyer specializing in LGBTQ matters can be an asset to your loved one.

An estate includes all of your loved one's assets including home, car, bank accounts, CDs, stocks, bonds, insurance policies, annuities, IRA/401K plans, and so forth. An estate plan includes legal documents such as a will, trust, power of attorney for financial matters, power of attorney for health care and living will, and the titles or beneficiary allocation for all of your assets. Many of your assets allow for beneficiary designations such as life insurance policies, bank accounts, stocks, annuities, real estate, and cars. Assets outside the will with beneficiary designations go to the beneficiary upon your passing and are not involved in probate. Even if a person does not intentionally create an estate plan, he or she has one by virtue of how assets have been titled and by the legal documents he or she has or does not have. This unplanned estate plan may not accomplish your loved one's goals.

A good estate plan allows a person to:

- control assets and property while alive and well
- establish a plan in case of disability
- give assets away as desired

While many families rely on sophisticated estate planning tools such as trusts and gift transfers to shelter assets from state or federal estate taxation, just about everybody stands to benefit from four basic estate planning tools, not only to arrange for the orderly transfer of assets to the next generation, but to plan for the possibility that at some point your loved one will be dependent on others to make important health care or financial decisions for him or her. These basic tools include:

1. **Last will and testament** to designate an executor for the estate, transfer assets, specify funeral or memorial wishes, or designate guardians for minor children.

    There are many types of wills to fit the needs of an individual. Below are the more common types of wills:

    Basic will: a basic or simple will that gives everything to a surviving spouse, children, or other identified heirs.

    Will with contingent trust: Commonly used by married individuals who have minor children who give everything to the spouse if living and, if not, to a trust for their minor children.

    Pour-over will: This type of will is usually used in conjunction with a living trust. It takes any assets that were not transferred to a trust during a person's lifetime and pours them into a trust upon death.

    Tax saving will: This type of will may be used to develop a testamentary credit shelter trust. This will allow lifetime benefits to a surviving spouse while not having those trust assets included in the survivor's estate at his or her subsequent death.

    Living trust without tax planning: Typically the surviving spouse has full control of the principal and income and the goal is to avoid probate.

    Bypass trust: This trust avoids probate and allows the first spouse to die to set aside monies in assets for specific heirs while continuing to provide income for the surviving spouse.

    QTIP trust: This trust allows the first spouse to die to be able to specify who will receive his or her assets after the surviving spouse dies.

2. **Durable power of attorney for financial matters** to manage money, including checking, savings, and investment accounts, and assets, including homes.

3. **Durable power of attorney for health care** to make medical treatment decisions. Sometimes, a health care power of attorney is also referred to as a "health care proxy."

    Note the distinction here between a "power of attorney" and a "durable power of attorney." Being designated as your loved one's general power of attorney allows you to perform tasks such as transferring a vehicle title, accessing a safe deposit box, hiring an accountant or lawyer, or simply for business-related purposes.

However, a power of attorney becomes ineffective if its grantor (your loved one, for example) dies or becomes incapacitated. A "durable" power of attorney enables you to act on their behalf in the event they become incapacitated.

If you are named as durable power of attorney it is important that you keep several copies of the document readily available as some entities will only accept an original.

4. **Living will** to specify wishes for continued medical treatment, such as life support, in case of terminal illness or permanent unconsciousness. A living will details preferences for medical treatment in life-prolonging procedures. This document becomes effective when an individual is in a terminal or unconscious state and contains two clauses regarding artificial hydration and nutrition as well as a Do Not Resuscitate clause.

It's a good idea to provide a copy of your living will to your physician for your medical file as well as a copy to anyone named on this document.

According to elder law attorney Margaret H. Kreiner, the most common estate planning mistakes are:

1. **You do no actual estate planning.** Your loved one's assets are titled without any thought about the future. Legal documents needed to accomplish estate planning goals such as a will, trust, power of attorney, power of attorney for health care, and living will are not executed or are not executed with attention to current goals. Estate planning should consider more than avoidance or minimization of estate taxes.

2. **No will is executed.** Without a will, assets will be divided according to state law. This may not coincide with your loved one's wishes.

3. **The wrong person is chosen to be the executor of the estate**. The executor will be responsible for the assets that pass according to your loved one's will. The person named as executor should be organized, detail oriented, and younger than your loved one. It may not be practical to name someone who lives across the country. Include one or two backup persons in case the first choice is unable or unwilling to be the executor. Make sure whoever is chosen to be executor understands his or her responsibilities and is willing to accept them. Being the executor of the estate can be a

stressful responsibility but one that needs to be well thought out. Even with all the estate planning in order, the executor needs to be fully aware of the loved one's wishes and be able to make decisions without emotions interfering in the process. Sometimes the primary caregiver is also the executor of the estate.

4. **Documents and beneficiary designations are not updated periodically.** Assets change as will family adjustments and the laws. Estate-planning documents (will, trust, powers of attorney, etc.) should be reviewed every three years and any time there is a major life change including marriage, birth of a child, or divorce, and any time a relevant law changes. Check beneficiary designations periodically to make sure these are current.

5. **Family is kept in the dark**. It is a good idea to explain your loved one's choices to his or her heirs so that they are informed. However, discussions are not legally binding. Often, family members fight over furniture, inexpensive jewelry, family photographs—not the things that you might think would cause a dispute. Consider advising your loved one to give away items while he or she is living. This allows your loved one to watch the enjoyment of the item.

The following information will be needed to prepare the basic estate documents:

- Name
- Address
- Social Security number
- Date of birth
- Length of time at residence
- Phone number
- Occupation
- Employer
- Marital status
- Prior marriages/details
- Information related to antenuptial or postnuptial agreements
- Children's names, ages, and dates of birth
- Spouse's name, age, and date of birth
- Parents' names, ages, and dates of birth
- Siblings' names, ages, and dates of birth
- Value of the following assets
    - Residence(s)
    - Household goods

- ▪ Jewelry
- ▪ Savings
- ▪ Retirement
- ▪ Automobiles
- ▪ Works of art
- ▪ Collectibles
- ▪ Annuities
- ▪ Other assets
- ▪ Life insurance
- ▪ Specific property bequeathed to a particular person upon death
- ▪ Gifts, and designated recipients
- ▪ Charitable donations
- ▪ Residuary estate designee(s)
- ▪ Designated executor of estate
- ▪ Durable general power of attorney
- ▪ Health care power of attorney
- ▪ Living will notice
- ▪ Designated guardian of your minor children
- ▪ Trustee (if applicable)

To help you gather this information, please see the following estate planning questionnaire provided by the law firm of Willis and Willis Co., LPA.

ESTATE PLANNING QUESTIONNAIRE

Information Needed	Client	Spouse
Full Name:		
Social Security Number:		
Date of Birth:		
Address: City, State, Zip:		
How Long at Residence:		
Home Phone Number:		
Occupation:		
Company:		
Business Phone:		
Martial Status:	☐ Single ☐ Married ☐ Separated ☐ Divorced	☐ Single ☐ Married ☐ Separated ☐ Divorced

(continued)

ESTATE PLANNING QUESTIONNAIRE *(continued)*

Information Needed	Client	Spouse
Prior Marriages to Whom:		

Describe below any agreement between you and prior spouse regarding property (antenuptial or postnuptial agreements). Please attach a copy of decree or dissolution and other documents regarding property settlement and custody of children.

Client	Spouse

Info. Needed	Client						Spouse		
	Name	Age	Birthdate	Name (or same?)	Age	Birthdate
Children:	1.			1.		
	2.			2.		
	3.			3.		
	4.			4.		
	5.			5.		
Parents:	Mother's Name and Address:			Mother's Name and Address:		
	Mother's Age or Date of Death:			Mother's Age or Date of Death:		
	Father's Name and Address:			Father's Name and Address:		
	Father's Age or Date of Death:			Father's Age or Date of Death:		

(continued)

	Name	Age or Date of Death	Name	Age or Date of Death
Siblings	1.		1.	
	2.		2.	
	3.		3.	
	4.		4.	
	5.		5.	

APPROXIMATE VALUE OF ASSETS

Items	In Client's Name	Joint? Yes or No	In Spouse's Name
Residences	$		$
Household Goods	$		$
Jewlery	$		$
Savings	$		$
Retirement	$		$
Automobiles	$		$
Works of Art	$		$
Collectibles	$		$
Annuities	$		$
Other (please list):	$		$

Life Insurance

Client		Spouse	
1st Policy	Company Name:	1st Policy	Company Name:
Company Address:		Company Address:	
Policy #:		Policy #:	
Face Value: $		Face Value: $	
Cash Value: $		Cash Value: $	

(continued)

ESTATE PLANNING QUESTIONNAIRE *(continued)*

2nd Policy	Company Name:	2nd Policy	Company Name:
Company Address:		Company Address:	
Policy #:		Policy #:	
Face Value: $		Face Value: $	
Cash Value: $		Cash Value: $	

Please list as completely as possible any specific property you wish to give to a particular person upon your death.

Client	Spouse
Gift to Name & Relationship:	Gift to Name & Relationship:
Gift:	Gift:
Gift to Name & Relationship:	Gift to Name & Relationship:
Gift:	Gift:
Gift to Name & Relationship:	Gift to Name & Relationship:
Gift:	Gift:
Gift to Name & Relationship:	Gift to Name & Relationship:
Gift:	Gift:
Gift to Name & Relationship:	Gift to Name & Relationship:
Gift:	Gift:

(continued)

Are there any charitable provisions you wish to make?	
Client	**Spouse**
Organization/Name:	Organization/Name:
Gift:	Gift:
Organization/Name:	Organization/Name:
Gift:	Gift:
Organization/Name:	Organization/Name:
Gift:	Gift:

To whom do you wish to leave your Residuary Estate?	
Client	**Spouse**
To:	To:
Percent:	Percent:
To:	To:
Percent:	Percent:
To:	To:
Percent:	Percent:
To:	To:
Percent:	Percent:
To:	To:
Percent:	Percent:

(continued)

ESTATE PLANNING QUESTIONNAIRE *(continued)*

Whom do you wish to name as EXECUTOR of your estate?			
Client		**Spouse**	
1st Choice	Name:	1st Choice	Name:
Relationship:		Relationship:	
Address:		Address:	
Phone Number:		Phone Number:	
2nd Choice	Name:	2nd Choice	Name:
Relationship:		Relationship:	
Address:		Address:	
Phone Number:		Phone Number:	
3rd Choice	Name:	3rd Choice	Name:
Relationship:		Relationship:	
Address:		Address:	
Phone Number:		Phone Number:	

To whom do you wish to give DURABLE GENERAL POWER OF ATTORNEY (if applicable)?	
Client	**Spouse**
Name:	Name:
Relationship:	Relationship:
Address:	Address:
Phone Number:	Phone Number:

(continued)

To whom do you wish to give HEALTH CARE POWER OF ATTORNEY?			
Client		**Spouse**	
1st Choice	Name:	1st Choice	Name:
Relationship:		Relationship:	
Address:		Address:	
Phone Number:		Phone Number:	
2nd Choice	Name:	2nd Choice	Name:
Relationship:		Relationship:	
Address:		Address:	
Phone Number:		Phone Number:	
3rd Choice (optional)	Name:	3rd Choice (optional)	Name:
Relationship:		Relationship:	
Address:		Address:	
Phone Number:		Phone Number:	

To whom do you wish to give notice in your LIVING WILL?			
Client		**Spouse**	
1st Choice	Name:	1st Choice	Name:
Relationship:		Relationship:	
Address:		Address:	
Phone Number:		Phone Number:	

(continued)

ESTATE PLANNING QUESTIONNAIRE *(continued)*

Client		Spouse	
2nd Choice	Name:	2nd Choice	Name:
Relationship:		Relationship:	
Address:		Address:	
Phone Number:		Phone Number:	

Whom do you wish to name as GUARDIAN of your minor children?		
1st Choice	Name:	Relationship:
Spouse's Name		
Address:		
Phone Number:		
2nd Choice	Name:	Relationship:
Spouse's Name		
Address:		
Phone Number:		

Whom do you wish to appoint as TRUSTEE of any trust (if applicable)?		
1st Choice	Name:	Relationship:
Spouse's Name		
Address:		
Phone Number:		

(continued)

2nd Choice	Name:	Relationship:
Spouse's Name		
Address:		
Phone Number:		

INVOLVE AN EXPERT

Navigating the legal arena in estate planning can be confusing for those of us who do not possess legal expertise. Knowing what is necessary to have created as a legally binding document may be out of your area of expertise, and the terminology can be confusing if you are not well versed in "legalese." In addition, the terminology, as well as laws for estate planning, differ from state to state. One family member shared that in the process of assisting her loved one in estate planning, she was advised that the loved one had to identify a relative in the state in which she resided to be the executor. In this state she was informed the courts would not usually grant this title to a relative who is out of state if there was a relative residing in the same state that could serve as executor. This is one example of how states may differ, and further assistance from a professional such as an attorney may be helpful in navigating through this process. (For further information specific to the state in which you reside, contact your local Bar Association for additional information. Many local Bar Associations have elder law committees which can provide expert advice based on the laws in your state.)

To ensure that your loved one's estate plan accomplishes his or her wishes, consult with an estate planning attorney, a CPA, and/or a financial advisor. Securing legal advice from a qualified professional, like an elder law attorney, can provide you with accurate and up to date information to assist you in making an informed decision and best prepare for your loved one's care.

ELDER LAW ATTORNEYS

Attorneys who are experts in elder law focus on the legal issues impacting the elderly population. There are many areas of elder law, so identifying the area in which you need most assistance and finding an attorney who specializes in this area are recommended. Examples of elder law areas of practice include:

- Estate planning
- Preservation/transfer of assets
- Medicare
- Medicaid
- Social Security
- Tax planning
- Assisted living/nursing home planning
- Financial planning
- Probate
- Long-term care
- Health law
- Mental health law
- Age discrimination in employment
- Elder abuse and fraud
- Supplemental and long-term health care
- Pre-burial planning

One caregiver shared her experience with an elder law attorney during which her elderly loved one's documents needed to be updated. Her elderly loved one was at a moderate to severe level of dementia and in an assisted living facility. She was frustrated with the process of having to sign her will, power of attorney, and other legal documents six years prior when her dementia was in the mild to moderate phase. The elderly loved one was now even more confused and often suspicious of potential changes in her life. Her caregiver was fearful that she would refuse to sign the necessary paperwork to update her estate planning and would become upset or combative.

The caregiver shared her concerns with the elder law office and was assured that as professionals working with elderly individuals daily, they understood these issues as well as the characteristics of individuals with dementia and would make every effort to ensure they communicated with her in a manner that did not cause her undue frustration or confusion. During the meeting, the eldercare attorney and her assistant quickly realized that the elderly individual was not able to sign her name on the documents due to her increased level of dementia. They explained the documents in a clear, concise manner and were able to accommodate her lack of ability through additional legal documentation.

Elder law attorneys focus their practice on working with the elderly and are familiar with the needs and issues of this population. Similar to geriatric physicians, elder law attorneys may often have a network of other geriatric professionals such as social workers or psychologists with whom they work. Elder law attorneys will assess your situation and advise you on options available to you.

CHECKLIST OF QUESTIONS TO ASK A POTENTIAL ELDER LAW ATTORNEY

- ☐ How long have you been in practice?
- ☐ How long have you focused on elder law?
- ☐ Do I need an eldercare attorney?
- ☐ What is your expertise in elder law, Medicare, and Medicaid?
- ☐ Are you certified in elder law?
- ☐ What is your length of experience?
- ☐ Have you had experience with other people in my situation or a similar situation?
- ☐ Are you an expert in the laws of this state?
- ☐ Do you belong to any other relevant organizations?
- ☐ Do you educate others about elder law (teacher or professor)?
- ☐ Are you a Super Lawyer?
- ☐ What resources can you provide related to elder law?
- ☐ What are the fees related to your services?
- ☐ Do you offer a free initial consultation?
- ☐ What information should I bring to the initial meeting?
- ☐ Should my elderly loved one attend the initial meeting?
- ☐ How many attorneys are in the office?
- ☐ Who will handle my case?
- ☐ What documents do I need to bring to the initial meeting?
- ☐ How long do you estimate we will work together?

ONCE YOUR DOCUMENTS ARE IN ORDER

Once you have executed an estate plan, it's important to keep these things in mind:

Maintain all these documents in a safe and secure location, preferably fire and waterproof. Inform pertinent family members so they can access these documents if necessary.

Review the estate plan documents annually to make sure they are up to date and reflect any status changes such as change in health, beneficiaries, birth of child, or death of an heir.

Inform pertinent family members of any changes to the estate.

~

Dani and Joseph's Experience with an Elder Law Attorney

Once Dani had confirmed with Dr. Shiloh that it was time to explore more skilled and full-time nursing care needs for Joseph, she immediately called a family meeting as the first step in this process. She discussed her concerns with her siblings and asked for their input as well. The first goal was to determine who would become Joseph's power of attorney for both financial and medical decisions. Since Joseph has been living with Dani, it was decided that she would act as power of attorney as she had been acting in this role unofficially for years. She was advised that determining a power of attorney for both medical and financial decisions should be the first step when exploring nursing care facilities.

Dani was unsure how to become Joseph's power of attorney, but after some Internet research, she found an attorney, Ms. Cremer, in her local area who specialized in geriatric legal needs. She set up a consultation with Ms. Cremer and Joseph. During this consultation, Ms. Cremer obtained the needed information and signatures to create the power of attorney documents. Ms. Cremer also informed Dani and Joseph that the Social Security Administration and Veterans Administration did not recognize legal power of attorney documents. The Social Security Administration has its own internal process to deem an individual the "payee" for a person receiving Social Security benefits. The Veterans Administration also has an internal process. Dani was also advised that as the individual who is overseeing veteran's benefits for her loved one that she should contact the social worker assigned to Joseph for further information.

Once the power of attorney documents and all other benefits had been designated, Dani made numerous calls on Joseph's behalf and was able to narrow down a list of facilities in the local area that took Joseph's insurance and provided the services that he needed.

Dani then began to identify skilled nursing facilities and scheduled appointments to tour them and meet with the administrators and staffs. She brought a checklist and questions so she would not forget to ask something. Dani also worked closely with Joseph's social worker at Veterans Affairs to assist in this process. Dani encouraged her siblings to take part in these meetings to assist in choosing an appropriate facility. When possible, she included Joseph in this process. However, due to Joseph's dementia and other disabilities, it was determined that bringing him to various facilities would only confuse and possibly upset him, so he was not part of most of the visits during the exploration phase of finding a skilled nursing facility.

Once a facility was secured, Dani completed all appropriate paperwork with the facility administrator and prepared to tell Joseph. Dani explained to Joseph that he was going to a rehabilitation facility to assist in making sure his medical needs were met and that he was in a safe environment. Joseph asked when he would come home and Dani told him that he would come home when it was safe for him to be there. Deep down, Dani knew the likelihood of Joseph regaining enough physical and mental strength to return home was not probable, but she felt that this was an honest answer because she would bring him home if it became an option to do so based on his medical, psychological, and cognitive functional abilities.

~

HEALTH CARE

New Medicaid rules took effect on October 20, 2006 making health care planning more important than ever before. The need to pay close attention to your elderly loved one's medical documents and health insurance coverage has never been greater given the changing nature of health care and health insurance in the United States. The reelection of President Obama in 2012 assured America that the Patient Protection and Affordable Care Act, also known as Obamacare, is here to stay. The constitutionality of most of this law's provisions were upheld in a June 2012 Supreme Court decision, and many of the reforms set forth in the Affordable Care Act were already in effect at the time this book was written.

Here are a few Obamacare provisions that are related to eldercare:

- Reducing the donut hole. Obamacare gradually reduces the amount that Medicare Part D enrollees are required to pay for their prescriptions when they reach the coverage gap.
- Expanding preventive health coverage. To increase the number of Americans receiving preventive care, Obamacare provides new funding to state Medicaid programs that cover preventive services for patients.
- Improving access to primary care. Obamacare requires state Medicaid programs to pay primary care physicians no less than 100% of Medicare payment rates for primary care services. The goal of this measure is to help ensure that there are adequate numbers of doctors available to treat Medicaid patients. This payment rate increase is fully funded by the federal government.
- Financial disclosure. Obamacare requires disclosure of financial relationships between health entities, including physicians, hospitals, pharmacists, other providers, and manufacturers and distributors of covered drugs, devices, biologicals, and medical supplies. This protects your elderly loved one by requiring health care providers to tell the patient in writing if they will make money from a drug or treatment they recommend.
- Higher spending caps. Before Obamacare, health insurance plans could set low annual limits on how much they would spend in total on a person's covered benefits. In 2013, Obamacare requires plans to provide no less than $2 million in annual coverage, and in 2014 the law entirely eliminates the ability of health insurance plans to impose annual limits of any amount. This is important—beginning in 2014, private insurers cannot cap the costs of your elderly loved one's health care—or the costs of anyone else's health care, for that matter!

Also under Obamacare, Medicare is increasing its payments for primary care doctors including family physicians, internists, and geriatricians. It will be reducing Medicare payments made to some specialists. Further, Medicare is instituting a new policy to pay a patient's physician or practitioner to coordinate the patient's care in the 30 days following a hospital or skilled nursing facility stay. This is known as

Transitional Care Management, and it could be a very important consideration for your elderly loved one.

Private insurance pays for very little skilled nursing care and Medicare pays for approximately 7 percent of skilled nursing in the United States. Medicaid is sometimes referred to as the only insurance plan for long-term care. Based on this information, as the caregiver, you should educate yourself about the types of care that may be available to your loved one to ensure he or she is getting all the benefits to which he or she is entitled. This step in and of itself will assist the Sandwich generation caregiver in the eldercare process.

Medicare is a government funded entitlement program that is generally available to people who are 65 or older, younger people with disabilities, and people with end-stage renal disease. Medicare provides health insurance with four different parts that assist in covering specific services.

Medicare Part A (Hospital Insurance) helps cover inpatient care in the following settings: hospitals, skilled nursing facilities, hospice, and home health care. Most people do not have to pay a premium for Medicare Part A because they or a spouse paid Medicare taxes while working in the United States. If an individual is not eligible for the premium-free Medicare Part A, there is an option to enroll and pay a premium.

Medicare Part B (Medical Insurance) assists with covering doctors' and other health care providers' services, outpatient care, durable medical equipment, and home health care, and helps cover some preventive services.

For Medicare Part B, most people do have to pay a premium. It is recommended that an individual obtain additional coverage that fills in the gaps in original Medicare coverage. There is an option to purchase a Medicare supplement insurance (Medigap) policy from a private insurance company.

Medicare Part C (also known as Medicare Advantage) offers health care plan options that are operated by Medicare-approved private insurance companies. Medicare Advantage plans are a way to get the benefits and services covered under Part A and Part B. Most Medicare Advantage Plans cover Medicare prescription drug coverage (Part D). Some Medicare Advantage Plans may include extra benefits for an extra cost.

Medicare Part D (Medicare Prescription Drug Coverage) assists with covering the cost of prescription drugs and may lower prescription drug costs and protect against higher costs. These plans are run by Medicare-approved private insurance companies and costs and benefits vary.

It is important to note that Medicare is an insurance plan in and of itself, and the supplements are optional for people who seek additional or broader based coverage.

If your loved one has limited income and resources, he or she may qualify for help paying for their Medicare health care and/or prescription drug coverage costs. According to the Social Security Administration (SSA), Medicare beneficiaries can qualify for Extra Help with their Medicare prescription drug plan costs. The Extra Help is estimated to be worth about $4,000 per year. To qualify for the Extra Help, a person must be receiving Medicare, have limited resources and income, and reside in one of the 50 states or the District of Columbia. The SSA recommends you apply for Extra Help on the Internet if:

- You have Medicare Part A (Hospital Insurance) and/or Medicare Part B (Medical Insurance); and
- You live in one of the 50 states or the District of Columbia; and
- Your combined savings, investments, and real estate are not worth more than $26,580, if you are married and living with your spouse, or $13,300 if you are not currently married or not currently living with your spouse. (Do NOT count your home, vehicles, personal possessions, life insurance, burial plots, irrevocable burial contracts or back payments from Social Security or Supplemental Security Income [SSI].)

For additional information call 1-800-MEDICARE (TTY 1-877-486-2048) or visit www.medicare.gov.

Medicaid is health coverage available to certain people and families who have limited income and resources. The rules for tallying income and resources such as bank accounts depend on which state you live in. Even if you aren't sure whether you qualify, if your income is limited, and if you or someone in your family needs health care, you should apply for Medicaid and have a qualified caseworker in your state look at your situation. People with Medicaid who are disabled or elderly may also be eligible for coverage for services such as nursing home care or home and community-based services. Each state has different rules regarding if a copayment for medical services is required. If you qualify for both Medicare and Medicaid, most of your health care costs will be covered, including prescription drug costs.

According to Medicaid.gov, Medicaid and CHIP provide health coverage to nearly 60 million Americans, including children, pregnant women, parents, seniors, and individuals with disabilities. In order to participate in Medicaid, federal law requires states to cover certain population groups (mandatory eligibility groups) and gives them the flexibility to cover other population groups (optional eligibility groups). Medicaid program.net states there are about 25 different categories of Medicaid eligibility. These can be grouped into five general Medicaid coverages that include people over the age of 65, children, pregnant women that have children, adults with dependent children, and people that are disabled.

While Medicaid eligiblity does vary by state, there are mandatory groups of people that do qualify no matter where they live. These mandatory groups include low-income families with dependent children, and women that are pregnant and have children and are below the federal poverty level. Also, beneficiaries of Medicare that have low income may also qualify.

Questions regarding Medicaid and eligibility should be directed to the appropriate State Medical Assistance (Medicaid) office for more information and specific eligibility criteria. Medicaidplanningassis tance.org is a website that can assist in determining one's Medicaid eligibility and also help in finding assistance qualifying and applying for Medicaid. While there are public employees that offer free assistance regarding Medicaid planning, one must meet specific eligibility criteria for this service. Private Medicaid planners are also available for hire. Medicaid planners assist families and individuals with the complexities of Medicaid eligibility. Medicaid planners are knowledgeable regarding specific state rules for eligibility as well as the application process.

If your loved one is in the process of becoming Medicaid eligible, the following information should be available to process the application:

- A copy of the authorized representative papers, power of attorney, or guardianship papers
- Social Security card
- Medicare card
- Birth verification
- Naturalization of alien registration if foreign born
- Marriage and/or death certificate of spouse
- Military discharge papers for client and/or spouse
- All liquid assets such as checking, savings, CDs, stocks, bonds, and so on

- Life insurance policies
- Proof of all income
- Proof of any income applied for such as VA benefits, Social Security Disability Insurance, and Supplemental Security Income
- Deed and property taxes for any assets
- Real estate listing agreement of property for sale
- Sales agreement of any property sold in the past three years
- Cemetery lot deed
- Title to vehicle(s)
- Supplemental hospitalization card, proof of premium, and address for claims
- Proof of spousal living expenses such as rent, mortgage, insurance, utilities
- Photo identification

Veteran's Benefits are provided by The U.S. Department of Veterans Affairs to veterans and their dependents. Veterans Affairs (VA) operates the largest integrated health care system in the United States with more than 1,700 sites of care, including hospitals, community health clinics, community living centers, domiciliaries, readjustment counseling centers, and various other facilities.

Eligibility for VA health care benefits are available for any person who served in the active military, naval, or air service and who was discharged or released under conditions other than dishonorable. National Guard and Reservist members may also qualify for VA health care benefits if they were called to active duty (other than for training only) by a federal order and completed the full period for which they were called or ordered to active duty.

The first step to confirm eligibility to obtain VA health care is to apply for enrollment. Enrollment can be completed online at the VA website, by calling the VA, or by visiting any VA health care facility or regional benefits offices.

Other. Your loved one may have health insurance provided by an employer, or if they are retired, have health benefits included as part of a pension. Educate yourself about the specifics of these policies.

Long-term care (LTC) insurance is an additional policy that may be purchased by an individual to cover costs that are not typically covered by traditional insurance or Medicare. Employers may offer these benefits as a group plan that may have multiple plan options for coverage. It is also offered by multiple insurance carriers.

And this is a companion spreadsheet used by the same caregiver to list his mother's income.

INCOME	
$1,119.00	DEPOSIT (SOCIAL SECURITY)
$624.29	DEPOSIT (PENSION)
$500.01	DEPOSIT (FINANCIAL SAVINGS)
$475.00	DEPOSIT (RENTAL)
$2,718.30	

As you can see when comparing the two spreadsheets, there is a discrepancy of more than $200.00 between what the elderly person's expenditures were on a monthly basis and her income. This illustrates the financial challenges that caregivers in the Sandwich generation often have in caring for their elderly loved ones.

Options that those in the midst of this situation might identify to cover the costs of eldercare include tapping into their children's college fund or compromising their own retirement savings. Prior to using resources set aside for a child's college fund, you should explore if your parent is eligible for Medicaid coverage or at what point he or she would become eligible for this government program. While parents of college-age students may want to tap into their retirement to help cover their children's college costs or assist in covering the long-term care of their elderly parents, financial advisors may advise otherwise.

While a college student can get a loan to assist in paying off education costs, it is more challenging to secure loans at the time of retirement. If one does not plan properly for retirement, he or she may ultimately end up depending upon their children for financial support. Grants and scholarships are an option that can be explored to assist members of the Sandwich generation who are confronted with having to pay for college costs of children while also trying to find ways to cover the cost of care for their parents. For the purposes of eldercare, using the assets of the parent or relative first and foremost is usually the most prudent for all involved. A reverse mortgage is one option to consider.

A good starting point for research on an LTC policy is at compare longtermcare.org. Things to consider and be prepared to answer when choosing an LTC policy include:

- Be aware that LTC policies typically are recommended for people who have considerable assets. Medicaid covers the expenses of those who have a small amount of assets.
- Determine how much coverage is needed. LTC policies typically pay $50 to $200 a day toward the cost of nursing facilities, in-home care, physical/occupational therapy, nurses' assistants and other health-related services.
- Confirm that the policy has a written guarantee that the policy won't be canceled or unrenewed as you age or become ill and that it will provide coverage for a minimum of a year or more.
- Ensure that the policy covers unskilled as well as skilled care.
- Confirm the policy doesn't require that you be hospitalized before you can receive your benefits for in-home or nursing facility care.
- Be aware that premiums will rise rapidly as you get older.

A comprehensive LTC policy will generally cover a wide variety of services needed, such as assisted living, respite care, hospice care, in-home care, skilled nursing facilities, and rehabilitation therapies such as speech, physical, or occupational therapy. Most policies require an elimination period, a period of time during which you must cover the cost of services prior to the LTC insurance becoming effective. A policy may also have limits based on the length of coverage as well as the amount of coverage provided.

Educating yourself about the benefits and shortcomings of LTC insurance will allow you to make an informed decision to determine if this is an option for you.

FINANCIAL

There are many facets related to overseeing your parent's finances. Filling out the Eldercare Plan document and estate planning will provide you with much of the information you will need to know. For example:

- If a power of attorney to manage their finances has been named
- Bank account numbers and names of financial institutions
- The name of their accountant or financial planner (if they have one)

Other information to gather includes:

- Location of financial records, including keys or codes to lock boxes or safes.
- Current monthly expenses, including mortgage, car payment, credit card debt, electric bill, and other expenses.
- How bills are currently paid: Are there automatic deductions being taken out of a checking account? Do they use online banking, or only paper checks?
- Annual income and sources: A monthly pension check? Social Security? Are dividends coming in from investments? Do they get money for a disability or alimony?

Even if you seem to have a complete list of accounts, double-check the list against tax returns and 1099 forms from payers as they come in.

In order to gain access to the accounts, pay bills, arrange for direct deposit of pension payments, or disbursements from investment accounts, you will either need to be named as a co-signer on the accounts (a joint account), power of attorney for financial matters, or guardian. Keep in mind that if you become a co-signer on the account, you become a "joint account holder," and the balance will transfer to you upon your parent's death.

To manage your loved one's Social Security benefits and/or SSI payments, you will need to be named as a Representative Payee. The SSA does not recognize a power of attorney for purposes of managing benefit payments.

Suggestions for easing the transition:

- One caregiver should be in charge but should regularly inform siblings or other pertinent family members in writing of what is going on, for example, quarterly reports, to prevent tension and disagreements.
- Put regular transactions on autopilot. Have Social Security and other monthly checks deposited directly into bank accounts and have utility bills automatically debited.
- Arrange to monitor accounts and pay bills online.
- Simplify where possible. For example, individual retirement accounts of the same sort can be consolidated.
- Keep detailed records.

Following is an example of a spreadsheet used by a caregiver to track his mother's expenses.

EXPENSES			
EXPENSES	**MONTH**	**QUARTER**	**YEAR**
PHONE/INTERNET	($70.71)		
MEDICAL CO-PAY	($40.80)		
CABLE	($66.87)		
NEWSPAPER	($20.00)	($40.95)	
SNOW PLOW SERVICES	($20.00)		($240.00)
LANDSCAPING	($20.00)		($240.00)
BANK (HOME EQUITY LOAN)	($407.09)		
INSURANCE (RENTAL PROPERTY)	($40.08)		
INSURANCE (HOME & CAR)	($100.00)		
GARBAGE (COUNTY DISP.)	($20.00)	($57.75)	
ELECTRIC	($54.40)		
GAS	($192.50)		
PROPERTY TAXES (HALF)			($220.27)
PROPERTY TAXES (HALF)			($201.04)
PROPERTY TAXES (HALF)			($17.01)
PROPERTY TAXES (HALF)			($293.53)
HOME COMPANION CARE	($880.00)		($5,143.00)
AARP (MEDICARE SUPPLEMENTAL)	($160.57)		
WATER	($20.00)	($52.42)	
MEDS	($650.00)		
GROCERIES	($200.00)		
	($2,963.02)		

REVERSE MORTGAGE

A **reverse mortgage** allows individuals 62 or older the opportunity to convert part of the equity in their home into cash without having to sell the home or pay additional monthly bills.

In a "regular" mortgage, monthly payments are made to the lender. In a "reverse" mortgage, money is received by the homeowner from the lender, and usually it does not need to be paid back as long as the homeowner continues to reside in the home. The loan is repaid when the homeowner is deceased, sells the home, or it is no longer his or her primary residence. The proceeds of a reverse mortgage generally are tax free, and most reverse mortgages have no income restrictions.

There are three types of reverse mortgages:

1. **Single-purpose reverse mortgages**, offered by some state and local government agencies and nonprofit organizations. This is the least expensive option but may not be available everywhere. This mortgage can only be used for one specific purpose and that is determined by the government or nonprofit lender.
2. **Federally insured reverse mortgages,** also known as Home Equity Conversion Mortgages (HECMs) and backed by the U. S. Department of Housing and Urban Development (HUD). These loans may be more expensive than a regular home loan and the upfront costs are usually high, but there are no income or medical requirements and the monies may be used for any purpose.
3. **Proprietary reverse mortgages** are private loans backed by the companies that develop them.

Reverse mortgage loan advances are not taxable, and generally do not affect Social Security or Medicare benefits. The homeowner retains the title to the home, and there are no monthly repayments, but again, the loan must be repaid when any of the following circumstances occur: when the last surviving borrower dies, sells the home, or no longer lives in the home as a primary residence.

In the HECM program, a borrower can live in a nursing home or other medical facility for up to 12 consecutive months before the loan must be repaid.

All options should be considered when determining if a reverse mortgage is the right decision. The following organizations have more information: the Federal Trade Commission, U.S. Department of

Housing and Urban Development (HUD), or the Reverse Mortgage Education Project, which is affiliated with AARP Foundation.

ELDERCARE FINANCIAL EXPERTS

Financial planning for eldercare has many nuances, so retaining a financial planner who is well versed in how finances and other factors such as Medicare, Medicaid, Social Security, and Veteran's Benefits may impact eldercare decisions is definitely worth considering. They can inform you of the availability of federal and state tax deductions and credits for people with disabilities, the elderly, and caregivers, and the pros and cons of claiming an elderly relative as a dependent, including various tax deductions such as eligible medical expenses and work-related expenses, including homecare or adult daycare.

There are two main types of eldercare financial experts:

An eldercare financial planner can help your family develop a long-term financial plan to maintain independence, maximize public assistance, make financial resources last longer, and preserve resources. In some cases, you can use the services of an eldercare financial planner in lieu of an eldercare attorney.

An eldercare financial consultant has the same qualifications as an eldercare financial planner but will not develop a financial plan for you. Rather, they will educate you and your family on how to develop a plan for yourselves.

Financial planners may also be known as charter life consultants, long-term care underwriters, or experienced certified estate planners.

Consulting with an expert in financial planning may assist in choosing the best option for your situation.

SENIOR REAL ESTATE SPECIALISTS

A home is often our most valuable asset. Another expert to consider as you review your elderly loved one's finances is a senior real estate specialist. These certified senior specialists understand the unique housing needs of the senior population. Not only can they assist when selling the family home, they can smooth the transition to the next home as they are aware of the financial and emotional challenges that face their elderly clients.

~

A Personal Story—Steve and Adaline

After Steve had successfully transitioned his mother to an assisted living facility, he wanted to be able to keep her there as long as possible. Financially, he was not sure he would be able to meet that goal based on her assets and income from Social Security and a small pension. He began to wonder if he and his wife needed to attempt to care for her in their home once her funds were gone. Being a dual income family with young children, this was not feasible.

Questions began to surface such as: Would Medicaid cover her in an assisted living facility once she became eligible for this program? Would they have to move her to a skilled nursing facility? Steve and his wife worried about what the future held for Adaline as they had finally transitioned her into an assisted living facility in which she felt safe, comfortable, and had developed a network of friends for socialization.

They consulted with an eldercare attorney who advised them on the process in their state that would allow her to stay at her facility once she became Medicaid eligible. What they found was that few assisted living facilities in their state accepted Medicaid vouchers. At the time they moved her from her home where she was living with home companion care, they were most concerned about transitioning her, and ensuring her level of care and ongoing support needs. They had not been focused on the long-term picture of what needed to occur to pay for her care in the assisted living facility once her money ran out. They were fortunate that the facility they chose did take Medicaid so that she could continue to remain in this facility once her funds were exhausted and she was Medicaid eligible. Had they been aware of this prior to placing her in the assisted living residence, they certainly would have taken this into consideration.

Steve also inquired about a reverse mortgage to liquidate funds for her care and was advised by an eldercare attorney that in order to be eligible for this, it had to be a primary residence. As she was now residing in the assisted living facility full time, he was able to rule this out as an option.

One factor that Steve and his family did consider when locating an assisted living facility for her was finding one that could care for her once she reached the next level of care. For example, the facility provided both assisted living as well as an Alzheimer's and dementia care specialty wing. With her diagnosis being dementia, he felt this was a good option as she could transition to that part of the facility if needed as her disease progressed.

Adaline's family began to work with the elder law attorney who visited Adaline in the assisted living facility to begin the paperwork process. Steve was concerned as Adaline was challenged when signing legal documents seven years earlier and her dementia was significantly greater at this time. The attorney and her assistant said that all Adaline had to do was make an "X" on the lines as she was unable to sign her name.

Adaline's family shared with her that some of her legal paperwork needed to be updated to allow Steve to continue to oversee her affairs, but also in an effort to preserve her assets to allow her to continue to live in the assisted living facility in the manner to which she had become accustomed. Adaline was comforted by this response, and although she was challenged with even making an "X" on the paperwork due to her physical limitations caused by the dementia, she was able to complete the process.

~

INVOLVING FAMILY MEMBERS

Making that initial step to get involved in your elderly loved one's care, or the step to make changes in the care that has already been arranged, can be a complicated proposition, but the transition process will be a better one if you and your entire family communicate honestly, cooperate without power struggles, and keep your elderly loved one's best interests and dignity at the heart of all decisions. One way to do this is to ensure everyone is in agreement on the final goal or outcome related to your loved one's care.

Involving family members in the planning process will ensure that everyone is aware of the options available and your loved one's wishes are followed when possible. Involving other family members is also a key component to making the preparation of care and estate planning as positive of an experience as it can be considering the decisions that will need to be made for your loved one. Reviewing all of the information above and determining the best route to take during estate and eldercare planning can be a draining and emotional experience. It is not a situation that most family members look forward to being part of, but it is a necessary step to ensure that the best route of care has been planned for your loved one.

Depending upon the relationships and dynamics of the family members involved, including everyone in the planning process may be challenging. Every family has its ups and downs and good and bad relationships. All of these issues need to be put aside and the focus needs to be for the benefit of your loved one.

Special care may be needed with blended families. With over half of marriages ending in divorce and over 75 percent of those individuals remarrying, blended families are becoming more of the norm and less of a minority. Oftentimes these blended families bring new issues and concerns to address on almost every topic. Where do the new family obligations fall, especially when this includes the caring of the loved one?

Many stepparents feel that they must walk a fine line with biological children of their spouse in order to keep the peace and/or a positive relationship. Stepfamily members may not feel the security or comfort level to address difficult situations or to reach out for help when needed. One woman stated that as the primary caregiver for her husband, who had been diagnosed with dementia and needed someone with him at all times, she felt uneasy asking her stepdaughter for help with her father. The stepmother did not feel she could really press the issue of how much she needed the stepdaughter's help. After the stepdaughter's repeated last minute cancellations of plans to take her father for the weekend and provide a break to her stepmother, the stepmother took matters into her own hands and paid for private caregiving so she could have a break from time to time. Would she have been more direct if it was her own daughter? Being aware of these potential issues and keeping the lines of communication open can help.

While email is a good way to document and plan, it can also be interpreted by some as being a cold and removed form of communication, so a mixture of all forms may be best. If family members are not in the same geographic area or are even in different time zones, email can be a good form of communication to use to allow all family members to provide input and feel as if they are contributing to the decision-making process. This also allows for time to "think things over" before providing a response to a question or comment.

Do's and Don'ts for Involving Family Members

Do

- Schedule a family meeting. With your loved one, gather family and friends involved in your loved one's care in person, by phone, or by web chat. Give everyone ample advance notice.
- Create an agenda for the meeting and distribute it ahead of time.
- Allow your loved one and other family members to share their thoughts, talk about how they feel about the options and this process, and then divide tasks that need to be completed.

- Identify someone to take notes and distribute to all family members following the meeting.
- Utilize resources of professionals and organizations that are expert in the services needed.
- Use an outside objective person to mediate if necessary, such as a counselor or clergy.
- Identify everyone's abilities as well as limitations in the caregiving tasks up front as this can make the planning and implementation process smoother.

Don't

- Threaten or use scare tactics.
- Guilt other family members into committing to assisting with your loved one's care. It will only cause problems and stress as time goes on and your loved one's needs increase.
- Feel like you have to be the only one in charge. Feedback and recommendations from other family members and professionals should be entertained.
- Make snap decisions when time allows for gathering information and resources and making an informed decision.

REVIEW YOUR PLAN

It is important to keep in mind that the eldercare, estate, health care, and financial plans that you and your loved ones create can change as your needs change. These documents are not written in stone, but they can be useful tools to help you and your family plan for the future. The details and information in these plans can assist at a time when emotions or timelines may not allow for a thoughtful and lengthy approach to decision making. By identifying this information prior to an immediate need, you have already put thought into options and can have a comprehensive approach to your loved one's long-term care needs. And remember, there are resources, like legal and financial professionals who specialize in eldercare needs, if you feel overwhelmed or uncertain, or think that expert advice is needed. These include:

- Elder law attorney
- Eldercare financial planner
- Eldercare financial consultant
- Senior real estate specialist

It's a good idea to review the following elements of your plan every year to make sure it is accurate and up-to-date, and always inform the relevant heirs and family members of any changes:

- Eldercare plan
- Estate plan
  - Will
  - Durable power of attorney for financial matters
  - Durable power of attorney for health care
  - Living will
- Health care
- Finances

Eldercare Strategy Do's and Don'ts

Do

- Incorporate your elderly loved one's feedback as well as other family members' recommendations whenever possible and appropriate.
- Gather comprehensive information including objective resources and data as well as subjective personal experiences to develop your eldercare strategies and plan.
- Identify eldercare strategies based on the individualized needs of you and your loved one.
- Remember that it is acceptable to alter your plan or strategy to meet the ongoing needs of your elderly loved one.
- Strive for excellence and not perfection in your eldercare strategies, as this may set you up to fail.
- Call upon experts for legal, financial, or medical advice when needed.
- Encourage family involvement in caregiving tasks.
- Take time for yourself.

Don't

- Hesitate to ask questions.
- Use cookie-cutter approaches to your individual eldercare strategies or plan.
- Wait until you are at a crisis stage to take action or develop a plan. This can reduce your options and place you in a reactive versus proactive position.

- Feel like you are alone—tap into resources available locally, by state or nationally.
- Make eldercare decisions based solely on guilt, emotions, or fear.
- Neglect yourself or other family members in your eldercare role.
- Focus on quantity of time with your loved one; make sure the time you spend together, even if it is limited, is quality time.
- Set unrealistic caregiving expectations for yourself or others.
- Use professionals who are not expert in eldercare services.
- Assume that what worked for other families will also work for you and your loved one.
- Be afraid to get a second opinion.

FOUR

Balancing Your Loved One's Wishes with Practical Reality: In-Home Care, Assisted Living or Skilled Nursing Facility, or Hospice Care

- Definitions and descriptions for each level of care
- Determine and choose the best care or facility
- Ease the transition

Once a caregiver has made the decision that his or her loved one needs more assistance and care than can be provided by himself or herself, even with the assistance of friends and family members, the next step is to determine what level of care is most appropriate to assist the elderly loved one in maintaining the highest possible level of independence, quality of life, and safety. In the vast majority of cases, the person's first choice is to remain at home for as long as possible.

IN-HOME CARE SERVICES

Care that is provided to a person at home has many names that include but are not limited to home care, home health care, and in-home care. These terms are used interchangeably regardless of the level of care that is required in the home. The goal of in-home care is to provide services that will make it possible for people to remain at home rather than relocating to a new residential setting where care is provided on site. Depending upon the person's needs and resources, in-home care usually consists of some combination of professional health care services and life assistance services. Professional health care services include medical and psychological assessment and treatment, wound care, teaching the person and his or her family how to administer medications, pain management, dietetics and nutritional consultation, disease education and management, physical therapy, speech therapy, and occupational therapy. Life assistance services are nonmedical supports that help the person perform activities of everyday life including meal preparation, walking, medicating, laundry, bathing and personal hygiene, using the toilet, dressing, light housekeeping, errands, shopping, transportation, and recreational activities, while also providing companionship. Life assistance services may also be referred to as companion care.

Genworth Financial's 2011 Cost of Companion Care Study estimates that in-home companion care averages $20.00 per hour in the United States. There are often minimum hour requirements for each visit as well as an expectation for notification of cancellations or schedule changes that need to be taken into consideration. It is common for in-home companion care providers to require a 24-hour advance notification of a cancellation or schedule change in order for the person to avoid being charged for the change in schedule.

Inviting someone you do not know into your home can be daunting. Inviting someone you do not know into your home to care for your elderly loved one is even more worrisome. Having an individual who is an independent contractor come into your home presents different considerations than using an agency or organization to provide these services. Obtaining information about the individual such as a background check, drug screen, and verification of credentials such as licensures, first aid, CPR, or other training would take place between you as the caregiver and the independent contractor directly. Payment to the independent contractor via a W-9 versus paying an agency or corporate service provider would also be a difference. A critical question to ask would be who would cover for the individual if he or she were sick or on vacation.

When using an agency for home health care services, we recommend always checking the agency's standing with the local Chamber of Commerce or Better Business Bureau before allowing them into your home.

QUESTIONS TO ASK WHEN RESEARCHING
A HOME HEALTH CARE PROVIDER

■ How do you screen your employees?

■ Do you perform background checks, drug screens, and tuberculosis testing?

■ What are the minimum training requirements for caregivers including First Aid training, CPR, and blood-borne pathogen training?

■ Does your agency require staff to have and maintain state licenses or certifications? If so, which ones?

■ How long have you been in business?

■ How many clients do you have? How many does each caregiver have?

■ How do you supervise the performance and quality of service of your providers?

■ Do you accept Medicare? Medicaid? My insurance?

■ Do you have an explicit LGBTQ nondiscrimination policy?

■ May I have two or three references?

Prior to the beginning of in-home services, an intake interview is usually conducted by the agency's Companion Care Management Team; at that time, you can set the parameters of the services that will be provided and what you can expect from the agency and its personnel. You should also establish:

Monitoring. How would you like to be kept informed? You may request that providers send a report of daily activities in a notebook or electronically via text message or email, including a log of any medication given. Or you may establish that you will call during the shift. Be specific about what you would like to know (eating patterns, mood, visitors, etc.) and how frequently you wish to be informed.

Consistency. Will the same caregiver tend to your loved one every day? This is often not the case. If your loved one is suffering from dementia or is otherwise calmed by consistency and routine, be sure to specify the need for a consistent caregiver.

Medication. How will medication be handled? Is the caregiver qualified to dispense medication? If not, what is the procedure? Your local pharmacy offers pill dispensing options that can be tailored to your loved one's needs, such as pre-dispensed foil packets containing all of the pills that are to be taken at a specific time during the day. The foil pouch is peeled back and can then be given to the individual if he or she has trouble opening bottles or is unable to take the medication unassisted due to safety concerns.

Procedure to deal with any problems, concerns, or an emergency. Establish a protocol for what should be done and who should be called if there is a problem or emergency. Make sure the caregiver and service know how to reach you and have all of your loved one's up-to-date medical information and contacts.

RESOURCES TO HELP YOUR LOVED ONE STAY AT HOME

Driving. If your loved one wants to continue to drive but you are concerned that he or she is not a safe driver anymore, a driving assessment may be a good way to obtain objective data from a professional to determine the reality of the situation. A driving assessment may even result in accommodations that allow your loved one to continue to drive.

A certified driver rehabilitation specialist (CDRS) is an expert, usually a driving instructor or occupational therapist, who is trained to evaluate someone's driving abilities. A CDRS may recommend driving cessation (or not) or safety devices, like special mirrors or adaptive foot pedals. If the CDRS concludes that an older adult can no longer drive safely, they will help ease the transition by providing concrete information and support.

Medical Alert or Senior Identification Tags. If your elderly loved one has a medical condition such as diabetes or dementia or has a tendency to wander, an identification tag may be helpful. This contact information tag offers peace of mind and personal safety, both of which are important for you and your elderly loved one at this stressful time for your family.

Medical alert systems such as Life Alert, LifeFone or LifeStation are designed to protect seniors as well as anyone else who needs an emergency response service.

Meals on Wheels. According to the Meals on Wheels Association of America, there are some 5,000 local Senior Nutrition Programs in the United States. These programs provide well over one million meals to seniors who need them each day. Some programs serve meals at congregate locations like senior centers, some programs deliver meals directly to the homes of seniors whose mobility is limited, and many programs provide both services.

~

A Personal Story: Adaline and Steve's Experience with Home Companion Care

In the case of Adaline and Steve, they needed someone to physically hand Adaline's medication to her. Living 90 miles away, Steve was able to prepare her prescriptions in a weekly medication container and place it in a location that was secure so that Adaline was unable to access it without assistance. The companion care provider gave her the medication from the container, thereby ensuring that Adaline took the prescribed doses of medication at the prescribed times. Because the companion care provider was not a licensed or certified medical professional, she was not allowed to dispense medication to Adaline. She was only allowed to hand the medication to Adaline after it had been pre-dispensed by Steve. Steve asked the provider to document the medications she handed to Adaline each day in a log book that Steve provided. This enabled him to monitor his mother's intake of prescribed medication.

Because of Adaline's dementia, Steve wanted to have consistency in the person who came to her home to provide companion care. Steve requested that the same woman be sent to Adaline's house each day. This was not possible all of the time due to vacations and days off, but the woman Steve selected as Adaline's primary companion care provider visited Adaline four to five days per week. Overall, the family's experience with in-home care was very positive, mostly because of the professionalism, trustworthiness, and kindness of the primary companion care provider and her colleagues. Steve maintained frequent contact with the staff, calling Adaline's home nearly every day to check in.

~

ASSISTED LIVING FACILITY

As the needs of your loved one increase, it may become time to consider the next level of care, an assisted living facility. Recall that Steve discontinued Adaline's in-home care after a few months and relocated her to an assisted living facility in his community. Having his mother nearby instead of 90 miles away enabled Steve to visit her every day and include her in a variety of family activities. The cost of Adaline's care was also a factor. At the time Steve made the decision to transition Adaline into an assisted living facility, 24-hour in-home companion care was costing $18 per hour or $432 per day. Adaline's out-of-pocket cost for the assisted living facility was less than $100 per day.

According to the U.S. Department of Health and Human Services, an assisted living facility is one that provides or coordinates oversight and services to meet residents' individualized scheduled needs, based on the residents' service plans, and their unscheduled needs as they arise. The Assisted Living Federation of America (ALFA) defines assisted living as a special combination of housing, personalized supportive services, and health care designed to meet the needs, both scheduled and unscheduled, of those who need help with activities of daily living. Assisted living usually includes 24-hour staff oversight, housekeeping, provision of at least two meals a day, and personal assistance services.

Assisted living facilities vary in the level of services they provide. States generally specify a minimum level of services that must be provided, but assisted living facilities determine the range of services offered, from those that are extremely limited (e.g., offering only one meal a day) to comprehensive services that can accommodate a high acuity level (e.g., skilled nursing care). What unifies assisted living facilities regardless of the definition one chooses is a wide range of services that cover a broad spectrum of resident needs, with services and supports being added to the service plan as the person's health and ability to perform activities of daily living decline. A hallmark of an effective assisted living facility is a willingness on the part of facility staff members and administrators to closely monitor each resident's progress and communicate openly with residents and their families to implement, evaluate, and modify needed supports over time.

As widely varied as state licensing and definitions are, so are the types of physical layouts of buildings that provide assisted living services. Assisted living facilities can range in size from a small residential house for one resident up to very large facilities providing services to hundreds of residents. In the continuum of care, assisted living falls somewhere between an independent living community and a skilled nursing facility.

People who live in newer assisted living facilities usually have their own private apartments. There is usually no special medical monitoring equipment such as one would find in a nursing home, and the nursing staff may not be available at all hours. However, trained staff members are usually on site around the clock to provide other needed services. Household chores such as changing sheets, laundry, cooking, and cleaning are provided. Meals are provided either in the person's living quarters or in a community dining room. Some facilities have beauty parlors and/or other amenities such as convenience shopping, pharmacy, and banking on site.

If private apartments are offered at an assisted living facility, they are usually self-contained and have their own bedrooms and bathrooms. Typically, these units have separate living areas and small kitchens. Other housing options may include a studio or suite apartment, where all amenities, including the kitchen, are located in one room. Other rooms in an assisted living facility may resemble a dormitory or hotel room consisting of a private or semi-private sleeping area and a shared bathroom. There are usually common areas for socializing, as well as a central kitchen and dining room for preparing and eating meals. Some assisted living facilities allow residents to have pets if they are able to care for animals on a daily basis.

Residents of assisted living facilities need not be concerned with daily meal preparation, because a central kitchen and dining facility typically provides three meals each day. Often, state regulations require that snacks be offered between regular meals. The central dining facility offers important opportunities for socialization as well, allowing residents to visit with one another and to receive guests. This greatly reduces the isolation and loneliness that elderly people often experience when they are living alone.

Residents are encouraged to take part in the community meals at assisted living facilities in an effort to increase socialization and nutritional intake. Assisted living facilities that provide in-room meals often assess an additional charge for doing so. Many facilities offer meals for visitors for a nominal fee in an effort to allow residents to enjoy meals with their families and friends.

An assisted living resident usually needs support with activities of daily living on a regular basis. Prospective residents are often assessed by the Director of Nursing or another medical staff member as to their level and type of need in the areas of bathing, grooming and hygiene, dressing, hearing, sight, speech, mobility, toileting, incontinence, laundry, medication, diabetes care, and meals and nutrition. Most assisted living facilities quantify the level and type of need identified for a particular prospective resident using a scoring system that is then compared to a fee structure to project the resident's expected costs. Once the resident moves into the assisted living facility, this assessment of service needs and costs is a fluid process so that the facility can monitor the person's service needs on an ongoing basis, make changes to the support plan as needed, and keep the person and his or her family members apprised of any changes in the costs of residence in the facility.

A typical assisted living facility resident is an elderly person who has significant companion care needs on a daily or regular basis but who does not need the intensive care of a nursing home. The Assisted Living Federation of America reported that the average age of assisted living residents is 86.9 years, with the average female resident being slightly older than the average male resident. Female residents outnumber male residents by a ratio of approximately 3 to 1, owing primarily to the fact that women have significantly longer life expectancies than men. The majority (76.6%) of assisted living residents are widowed, with only 12 percent still married or with a significant other. The average length of stay for an assisted living resident is just over 2 years—28.3 months.

~

A Personal Story: Steve and Adaline's Experience with an Assisted Living Facility

Steve's first experience with the facility he ultimately chose for Adaline was very positive. Upon his arrival, he was approached by a friendly staff member who welcomed him and asked how she could assist him. Many of the residents were in the lobby area interacting with each other and the staff. He immediately detected a strong sense of community and a warm, nurturing atmosphere. Steve felt welcome in the facility, but he was also impressed by security measures such as punch codes to open doors that allowed people to enter or exit the facility.

Steve found the proximity of the assisted living facility, within walking distance of his home, to be a major advantage. He knew that this would allow him and his family to visit Adaline often and closely monitor her adjustment to her new surroundings. He was impressed by the wide range of social and recreational activities offered by the facility, and he learned that the facility enjoyed low staff turnover, with many people who had been employed there for years. He met with the marketing coordinator, who answered all of his questions and invited him to stop by anytime to observe. She also invited him to come to Family Night to see one of the activities they offered. Steve was assured that he and his family could visit Adaline in her apartment whenever they wished to, and that Adaline would not be restricted from visiting Steve's home or other locations in the community.

Steve and his family also liked the fact that they could decorate Adaline's apartment the way she liked it, including painting. Her quarters offered a private bath but no kitchen, and Steve provided a small refrigerator that he kept stocked with Adaline's favorite soft drinks and snacks. The facility offered a galley kitchen with a refrigerator and microwave on each wing, as well as one full kitchen made available to residents and their families on a reservation basis.

~

SKILLED NURSING FACILITY

Skilled nursing facilities provide a home for people whose medical and/or psychological conditions require around-the-clock care by skilled nurses. Skilled nursing facilities also provide therapy and rehabilitation services for people with disabilities of any age, all in an effort to help people live more comfortable lives. These facilities are for people who require more intensive care and support than people living in assisted living facilities, and residents of skilled nursing facilities may live there on a short-term or long-term basis.

A skilled nursing facility is appropriate for people who are very ill or who need to recover from serious accidents or surgeries. Specialized therapies are provided on site, and assistance is available on a 24-hour basis to help residents with activities of daily living.

~

A Personal Story: Joseph and Dani's Experience with a Skilled Nursing Facility

When Joseph's needs made it impossible for Dani to care for him in her home any longer, it became evident that he needed the support of a skilled nursing facility, also known as a nursing home. Although Dani did not want to admit it, Joseph required professional medical services on a 24-hour basis. His dementia and his other medical and psychiatric needs were too advanced for an assisted living facility. Signs that Joseph needed the 24-hour care of a skilled nursing facility included his inability to manage his medication regimen, falling on the floor because he could not remember that he was unable to walk, and irrational outbursts of anger that were not prompted by any particular stimulus (i.e., getting angry for no apparent reason). One of Joseph's falls sent him to a local Veterans Affairs (VA) hospital to recover from his injuries.

During Joseph's stay at the veterans' hospital, Dani began to inquire about the next steps in coordinating his transition to a skilled nursing facility. Dani received a telephone call from a Veterans Affairs (VA) social worker who identified herself as Joseph's case worker, Jane. In all the years that Dani had been overseeing Joseph's care, she had never known he had an assigned social worker. Jane informed Dani of the VA benefits to which Joseph was entitled, which included 100 percent paid coverage at a skilled nursing facility because Joseph had been certified as 100 percent disabled by the VA. Jane then provided Dani with a list of skilled nursing facilities in her local area that accepted VA benefits. Dani shared this list with her family, and she found that a family friend worked at one of the facilities on the list. Dani's friend had many positive things to say about her employer and the services offered at the skilled nursing facility, and she introduced Dani and Joseph to administrators and staff members of the facility.

Dani visited the facility where her friend worked and two other skilled nursing facilities on the list. Dani was impressed by all three facilities and believed that her father would be well cared for and comfortable at any of the three facilities. After learning that the other two facilities were not accepting new residents at that time, Dani arranged to have Joseph placed at the facility where her friend worked. Jane and the medical staff of the VA hospital were tremendously helpful in helping Dani with Joseph's transition to the skilled nursing facility, and Jane visited Joseph and Dani regularly at the facility to monitor his progress and provide any needed assistance.

~

CONTINUING CARE RETIREMENT FACILITY

Continuing care retirement facilities combine independent living, assisted living, and skilled nursing care in one comprehensive program. If you know that your loved one's medical or psychological condition is progressive and that he or she will likely need to transition to more intensive supports in the future, you may want to find a continuing care facility to ease the transition from one level of care to the next. Some continuing care facilities have levels of care from cluster homes and condominiums to skilled nursing. Some families choose these locations because the resident can receive the care he or she needs while retaining his or her comfort with the overall location and the amenities of the program itself, rather than relocating to different facilities altogether as his or her needs progress. Another benefit of continuing care retirement facilities is that family members are familiar with the culture, environment, and even staff of the facility, thereby making the transition more palatable for them as well.

SELECTING A FACILITY

Once you have made the decision regarding the type of residential facility that your loved one needs, it is time to research specific facilities in the community to narrow down the selection. You can begin to search for assisted living facilities or skilled nursing facilities via the Internet. The U.S. Department of Housing and Urban Development (HUD) is also a good resource. There are numerous criteria to consider when choosing a facility and the checklist on page 90 will help you obtain the detailed information necessary for you to make a decision. There are three major areas of consideration:

Provides Necessary Care in a Safe Environment: Make sure the facility is able to meet *all* of your loved one's health care needs with the appropriate levels of staff. Additional qualities to consider include:

Security: Although you want to be able to visit your loved one freely and without restriction in his or her new place of residence, you also want to know that he or she is safe and secure. This assurance requires strict procedures for monitoring visitors and residents as they enter, move through, and exit the facility. You may also want to ensure that there is a secure mechanism in place so that those with dementia or Alzheimer's who may wander from their rooms are prevented from exiting the facility without someone available to assist them.

Attends to Personal Safety: The unique personal safety concerns of your loved one need to be monitored. An example of this may be a recommendation to purchase shoes that use Velcro instead of laces if the facility finds that your loved one is unable to tie his or her shoes and the laces have become a safety issue.

Health monitoring and communication: Inquire about the facility's procedures for communicating information about a person's health status and functional abilities. Many disabilities are invisible or not readily apparent. This is true for many of the conditions that affect the elderly. Alzheimer's and dementia may not always present themselves in a manner that would allow someone who is not familiar with the person to know that he or she has one of these diagnoses.

Financial: Do you or your loved one have the resources to pay for the facility over the long term? It's important to consider how the facility will be paid, if the facility accepts your loved one's long-term health insurance, Medicare, and Medicaid. Useful long-term care resources include:

- **Longtermcare.gov**: Sponsored by the U.S. Department of Health and Human Services, provides information and resources to help families plan for long-term care and provides information on paying for long-term care that is not covered by Medicare and can be very costly.
- **Your state's long-term care website** for assisted living and skilled nursing information, including whether or not a facility accepts Medicaid.

Quality of Life: To determine the quality of life of residents at the facility you are considering, it is essential for you or someone in your family to physically visit the facility during "announced" visits such as a formal tour as well as stopping by "unannounced." Stopping by "unannounced" will give you an idea of what is happening at the facility at any given point in time. Checking in at nontraditional times such as during evenings or weekends will give you an idea of staffing and activity levels outside of the normal eight-to-five workday. Many facilities have administrative, therapy, and other staff available during the normal work week, but staffing levels on the weekends are often reduced. Unannounced visits to the facility are one way to evaluate the services and culture of the facility in its natural state.

During your visits, speak to current residents to find out about their experience. Attend a family council meeting or ask a facility administrator to connect you with a family member of a current resident to interview them about their experience with the services, programs, and care of the facility. Family council meetings generally occur within an assisted living or skilled nursing facility at least monthly to allow residents and family members a forum to communicate about any recommendations or concerns they may have related to the care provided by the facility. Family councils also provide support and information to residents and their families.

Other ways to visit:

Trial visit: Some facilities allow prospective residents to stay at the facility for a few days on a trial basis before making a final decision.

Participate in adult day care programs or respite care programs:
These are a good way to try out the facility on a temporary basis.

Participate in community outreach activities: Activities like egg
hunts for children in the spring, holiday events in the winter,
and other activities such as family nights and open houses
will allow you to observe the activities and environment up
close and obtain a clear indication of the culture of the facility.
Facilities that partner with local schools, churches, and other
community organizations allow increased opportunities for
residents to engage in their communities, and this also provides transparency through which the community can observe
the services and activities of the facility.

Volunteer: Spending time in an assisted living or skilled nursing
facility can also give you important perspectives on the activities, services, policies, and procedures of the facility.

Karl Zalar has been a nursing home administrator for more than
15 years. He recommends the following Do's and Don'ts when selecting
an assisted living or skilled nursing facility for an elderly loved one.

Do

▓ Take a comprehensive facility tour to hear staff interact with
residents and see what people are doing in activities and care. A
15 minute walk-through will not always provide the family or
elderly loved one the information needed to make an informed
decision about a facility.

▓ Be very cautious about hidden charges when shopping for an
assisted living or skilled nursing facility. Some facilities have a
base fee and charge extra for everything else. Know hidden costs
or charges such as medication administration. There are often
"a la carte" charges. Ask about what charges are involved in the next
level of care. Some people come in under the (mistaken) assumption
that the level of care cost is static and does not increase. Costs often
increase when a resident becomes more dependent upon the facility
staff for assistance in completing activities of daily living.

▓ Understand the financial liability of the resident regardless of whether
he or she has financing. Medicaid does not pay for everything.
Resident liability requires that the person has to turn over resources
remaining after going through the Medicaid spend down. Once

an individual is a Medicaid recipient, any Social Security, pension, or other income, with the exception of approximately $50.00 per month, must go toward his or her assisted living or nursing care. As mentioned previously, each state has different criteria for Medicaid eligibility, but an applicant must have minimal assets (usually less than $1,500.00) in order to be eligible for this program.

- Get everything in writing when searching for a facility. Families are often in a stressful situation during this time and getting information in writing will allow for further review during the decision making phase, and help in ensuring that expectations are met if and when your loved one becomes a resident of that facility.
- Ask about employee turnover rates. The American Health Care Association conducted a study of nursing home turnover in 2007, revealing vacancy rates among staff RNs and LPNs were 16 percent and 11 percent, respectively. The level of turnover among nursing assistants was of particular concern at 66%.
- Ask to see the last state survey. A state survey is conducted to evaluate quality of care and service provided by a skilled nursing facility based on state and federal laws and rules. Other areas investigated may include complaints related to residents' rights, quality of care, quality of life, staffing, abuse, and dietary and environmental concerns.
- Check out the Centers for Medicare and Medicaid Services (CMS) website (www.cms.gov) that allows you to compare up to three nursing homes side by side by a five-star rating category. The last three state surveys are also available on this website.
- Look at your state's long-term care website for nursing home information that provides the latest resident and family satisfaction surveys. For example, in Ohio it is www.LTCohio.org. These websites will also tell you how many beds are in the facility and if they take Medicaid.
- Consult with an eldercare attorney who has a clear understanding of state Medicaid law and regulations.
- Obtain a copy of the facilities "Residents' Rights."

Don't

- Take everything in the online Nursing Home Comparison at www.cms.gov at face value. You must still take the information you get on this site, set up a comprehensive tour of the facility, and ask detailed questions.

QUESTIONS TO ASK WHEN RESEARCHING ASSISTED LIVING OR SKILLED NURSING FACILITIES

General

- Is the facility certified/accredited?
- What is the average number of residents?
- What is the maximum number of residents?
- What is the staff-to-resident ratio?
- Does the staff seem to have a positive relationship with the residents?
- What is the staff turnover in the facility?
- Has the facility received any awards or recognition from state or local agencies?
- What is the cost of care monthly?
- What insurance does the facility accept?
- Can residents share rooms?
- Are pets allowed?
- Are personal toiletries (toothpaste, shampoo, soap) provided by the facility?
- Do rooms have their own temperature controls?

Health Services and Specialty Care

- Does this facility provide the level of care needed for my loved one?
- Does it specialize in the diagnosis my loved one has, such as dementia, Alzheimer's, Parkinson's, and so on?
- Can residents still see their own personal doctors?
- Does the facility provide pharmaceutical services?
- Does the facility provide or coordinate transportation for activities as well as medical appointments?
- Does the facility have a relationship with a nearby emergency room/hospital and/or urgent care center, and is there close access to emergency transportation services?
- Does the facility have an automated external defibrillator (AED)?
- Is there a licensed nursing staff 24 hours per day?
- Does the facility provide pet therapy and physical, occupational, or speech therapy?
- Is respite care available at this facility?
- Does this facility have a continuum of care?

Facility Policies, Procedures, and Requirements

- Does the facility complete background checks and drug screens on all employees?
- What security mechanisms are in place for residents who may wander?
- Is there security to monitor visitors?
- Does the facility have an emergency evacuation plan?
- What procedures are in place for fire, tornado or natural disaster, utility failure, bomb threat, or other types of emergency?
- What are the minimal training requirements for staff (e.g., CPR, first aid, and blood-borne pathogens training)?

Activities, Social Interaction Opportunities, and Family Involvement

- Is the facility centrally located so that family and friends can visit easily?
- Does the facility offer family or community events?
- Are family members able to stop in at any time of day or night?
- What amenities are on site (e.g., salon, bank, convenience store, garden)?
- How often are residents assisted with showers/bathing, laundry, and housekeeping?
- What community areas are available for watching television and other recreation?
- Is there a community kitchen available to residents?
- Do resident rooms have kitchens?
- Are refrigerators or microwaves allowed in resident rooms?
- Are residents allowed to smoke in designated areas?
- Are there private or quiet areas where residents may visit with friends and family?
- Do all areas provide accommodations for wheelchairs?
- Are residents allowed to have televisions and radios?
- Are there regular activities for the residents to participate in, such as bingo, card playing, book reading, jigsaw puzzles, and exercise groups?
- Does the facility coordinate field trips to a zoo, park, museum, movie theater, restaurant, or retail shopping?
- Is there a formal volunteer program? What are the screening procedures?

- Are family members allowed to volunteer?
- Are there outdoor areas for the residents to utilize?
- Does the facility provide religious services?
- What does the meal plan entail? Are visitors welcome during meals and if so, what is the fee?
- Are residents able to order from a menu or are multiple meal options available at each meal?
- Are residents able to paint or decorate their own rooms?
- Does the facility hold a resident and family council meeting regularly?
- Can residents assist with activity and meal planning?
- Is cable or phone service available, and if so, how is it set up?
- Is wireless Internet access available?
- Is there an exercise room or workout facility?
- Are refreshments available for residents and guests, such as coffee, tea, and so on?
- Does the facility have a library or movies available for checkout by residents?
- Does the facility provide a newsletter and monthly calendar of events?
- How are residents recognized for birthdays, Veterans Day, anniversaries, resident of the month, and so on?
- Are there special activities on holidays?
- Are music and entertainment available regularly?
- Is there a café or are there vending machines on site?
- What crafts or leisure activities are available?
- Is there a piano/organ or other instrument on site?
- Is there a webcam available on site?
- Can families spend the night?
- What are the procedures to take your loved one out of the facility?
- How is mail service handled?

For LGBTQ Seniors

- Does the facility have an explicit LGBTQ nondiscrimination policy?
- Does the facility currently employ any "out" LGBTQ people or currently serve any "out" LGBTQ clients?
- Have staff members been trained by a local LGBTQ elder advocacy organization?

- Does the facility display LGBTQ symbols or literature or include LGBTQ-welcoming materials among their brochures?
- Are intake forms and marketing materials LGBTQ-inclusive? (For instance, do forms for new residents include a place to note a same-sex partner?)
- Do they allow same-sex couples to live in the same room?
- Does this agency support "families of choice" in their policies and programs (i.e., friends and others who are the main sources of support for many LGBTQ elders)?

A 2011 report conducted by a broad coalition of LGBTQ groups led by the National Senior Citizens Law Center found that nearly nine in ten respondents said that they thought long-term care staff would discriminate against someone who came out in a facility; eight in ten responded that they would expect mistreatment or bullying from nursing home residents; and one in ten reported that nursing home staff had disregarded a medical power of attorney when it was assigned to a resident's partner. Transgender elders in particular reported that they experienced isolation and staff refusal to recognize their gender identities.

Another study, completed by Mark Hughes of the University of Queensland, Australia, concluded that nearly two thirds of participants felt that their sexuality or gender identity could affect the eldercare services provided to them. Many predicted that they would, in fact, be discriminated against in receiving eldercare services or that their same-sex relationship would not be recognized in an eldercare assisted living or nursing facility setting.

Staff training is vitally important when it comes to LGBTQ issues. By mandating it, management and other leaders in institutional facilities make clear that anti-LGBTQ discrimination will not be tolerated. To find an organization to conduct training at a facility near you, contact your LGBTQ community center, local or state-wide Equality Federation organization, SAGE (www .sageusa.org), or look for resources on the National Resource Center on LGBT Aging (www .lgbtagingcenter.org).

There are legal protections for LGBTQ elders. At the state and municipal level, LGBTQ-inclusive nondiscrimination ordinances that cover public accommodations should also cover long-term care facilities. At the federal level, the Nursing Home Reform Act and the Federal Housing Act also may provide protections. State tort laws, nursing home rights laws, and other legal protections also provide important tools for advocates. For an individual case, you should contact an advocacy organization for an assessment.

HOSPICE CARE

Hospice care is provided to an individual who is at the end of his or her life. Generally, individuals are referred to hospice to address pain and symptom control when they are expected to live six months or less. Hospice care can be provided in an assisted living facility, a skilled nursing home, a hospice care facility, a hospital, or the person's home. Hospice provides medical, psychological, and spiritual support to individuals in an effort to allow them to die with peace, comfort, and dignity. Hospice services also assist the caregiver in preparing for and maintaining the caregiver role at the end of the elderly loved one's life.

Services provided by hospice staff generally include regular visits by a registered nurse; mental health and/or pastoral counseling; and physical, occupational, speech, music, massage, and art therapy. Hospice services can assist with the purchase or rental of medical equipment and supplies for the home such as a hospital bed, wheelchair, bedside commode, and other durable medical equipment. Other services available through most hospice programs include grief and family counseling, bereavement support, social worker services, and chaplain services. Hospice services are typically covered by Medicaid, Medicare, or private insurance.

Hank Dunn, hospice chaplain and author of *Hard Choices for Loving People*, states that the four most common decisions that need to be made by patients nearing the end of their lives and by their families are:

- Should resuscitation be attempted?
- Should artificial nutrition and hydration be utilized?
- Should a nursing home resident or someone ill at home be hospitalized?
- Is it time to shift the treatment goal from cure to hospice or comfort care only?

Dunn also notes that patients and families participating in hospice care need to consider the goal of medical treatment. Goals for medical care can include the prevention or cure of the disease, stabilizing or inhibiting the disease from worsening, and preparing for a comfortable and dignified death.

The American Cancer Society is an excellent resource for families seeking hospice care. The Society recommends asking the following questions when searching for a hospice program:

- Is the hospice program accredited, certified, or licensed to meet minimal standards of care?
- Does the agency provide information on services, eligibility, treatment limits, and costs that can be provided to aid in your decision-making process?
- Are references available for the program as well as the personnel?
- What is the admission process? Is an initial evaluation completed? By whom?
- Does the agency develop a plan of care for each patient as well as a plan for emergencies such as a power failure or natural disaster?
- Does the agency require that a patient have a primary caregiver?
- Does the agency provide inpatient, hospital, or in-home care?
- What are the patient's rights and responsibilities?

MAKING THE TRANSITION EASIER

Although there are many differences between raising children and caring for an elderly loved one, the presence of competent and loving caregivers is the most important factor in both endeavors. Many of the lessons that parents learn in caring for their children translate well to eldercare, especially those decision-making skills that protect the safety and comfort of loved ones. One member of the Sandwich generation told us that she employed similar strategies to find her mother an assisted living facility as she had employed several years earlier in selecting a day care program for her children. And she noted that the day she brought her mother to live at the assisted living facility brought back memories of leaving her children at day care for the first time.

It can be an emotionally taxing proposition to entrust the care of loved ones, be they children or adults, to other people. Just knowing that you will experience strong emotions when you must make a change in your elderly loved one's living and care situation helps to prepare you and your family for the transition, but finding ways to process and deal with those emotions is very important at this time. Talking, either with a friend who has been through this situation or at a support group is one way to work through these emotions. Another option is to speak with a counselor or a member of the clergy as part of the transition. Keeping a journal can also be a powerful way to sort out and internalize painful and conflicting emotions.

Use your care team as a support and resource. In the case of Joseph and Dani, there were many details regarding Joseph's benefits that Dani had not been aware of even though she had been his primary caregiver for several years. Using the social worker as a resource and support mechanism was helpful in the transition process for Joseph, Dani, and their family. Joseph's medical team was very helpful as well, and it gave Dani great comfort that her friend had an insider's perspective on the skilled nursing facility she ended up choosing for her father. Dani found that asking questions was the best way for her to develop a plan for Joseph's transition to a more advanced level of care.

Honor your loved one's choice as much as possible. Balancing your loved one's expectations with practical reality is a challenging proposition. Identifying your loved one's expectations is the first step in attempting to strike this important balance. Your elderly loved one may feel that his or her choices are being restricted as his or her needs for care increase, and this may be true to some extent. That said, it is important to honor your elderly loved one's prerogative and choice to every extent possible in deciding the most appropriate care and residential setting for him or her. The skills we in the Sandwich generation employ in developing decision-making abilities and independence in our children become important as we help our parents and grandparents strike the delicate balance between their wishes and practical reality. Sometimes we have to go against our children's expressed desires for their own good, and the same issue arises in eldercare decision making. Involving your elderly loved one to every extent possible in the decisions that affect him or her, consulting objective resources in making decisions, and communicating honestly and openly with your elderly loved one and all family members are the best ways of making sound decisions that reflect as much input from your elderly loved one as possible.

Sometimes it is necessary for you as the caregiver to determine a fixed set of possible choices regarding your elderly loved one's care, all of which you have already determined to be feasible options. Then, you may ask your elderly loved one to choose from the pre-determined set of options. Your elderly loved one has the opportunity to exercise choice, and the choice he or she makes in this scenario is, by definition, one that you and your elderly loved one agree on. We are reminded of the choice that parents often offer to their children, "Would you rather clean your room before doing your homework, or would you rather do your homework before cleaning your room?"

Balancing the reality of your situation with your loved one's wishes is an ongoing task that is fluid as circumstances change, including your loved one's physical, emotional, psychological, and financial status.

Make the transition to assisted living or a skilled nursing facility as slowly as possible. Consider respite care programs that enable your loved one to stay at home as long as possible—chances are that is what he or she wants.

But don't alternate between facility and home care for your loved one. This does not allow for structure or an opportunity for him or her to feel comfortable in one place. Your elderly loved one might find it confusing or disorienting to be frequently transported back and forth between part-time residences.

Address your loved one's fear of isolation. Another concern that your loved one may have is fear of isolation from family and friends if he or she were to move to an assisted living or skilled nursing facility. The reality of moving your elderly loved one to a facility is that he or she may become even more socially active than he or she would have been if continuing to live alone. One member of the Sandwich generation joked that, after moving his mom into an assisted living facility and seeing her social activity increase, her new environment, "was like a college experience." Although his mother had worried about becoming isolated and lonely, the reality was that she was busier and more socially involved than she had been in the previous five years when she lived alone at home. After just over one year in her new home in the assisted living facility, she had developed dozens of friends, participated in community outings on a weekly basis, enjoyed on-site church services, and was crowned "Valentine Queen." She admitted she was happier in her new home in the assisted living facility than she had been in years. Her fear of isolation and loss of independence quickly faded as she felt safer and more secure in her new home.

Be aware of the health of your healthy parent if one parent is ill and the other is not. Make sure you provide respite for your healthy parent so the stress of caregiving does not burden him or her and affect his or her health negatively. When a parent's health declines it shakes the foundation of a family and may change the daily routines and way of life forever. The healthy parent will have to begin taking on more household responsibilities, and this may be emotionally draining as well as take a physical toll on the healthy parent. Both parents may start to feel powerless about the situation. This sense of vulnerability may lead to depression, feelings of anger, and moodiness in both the healthy and the sick parent.

Stay in touch. One of the most important issues families face during these transitions is finding ways to stay in touch with the person who is moving to another location and level of care. If you cannot visit your elderly loved one in person as much as you would like to, providing him or her with a cellular phone and/or a landline in his or her new living quarters is a good way to keep in touch. There are many devices and accessories that can help elderly people make full use of the telephone to communicate with family and friends. These include enlarged keypads for both cellular and landline phones, some of which allow a picture of an individual to be placed under a particular key and will dial that person's number when pushed.

Plan family and community events. Making arrangements to take him or her out to community or family events is beneficial for you and your loved one. You may find that you have more opportunities to spend quality time with your loved one once you transition him or her into the assisted living or skilled nursing facility because you are no longer singlehandedly overseeing his or her care on a daily basis. If your loved one can be easily transported, going out shopping, for a meal, or to a movie is a good way to meet his or her needs for socialization. Events could be as simple as going for ice cream or coffee or to a grandchild's pre-school show, or even just visiting a local park.

Most modern facilities offer family recreational areas that allow for parties and social gatherings. Planning a gathering or regular family dinner at the facility is another good way to alleviate your loved one's fears of loneliness while permitting him or her to host social events if that is something he or she did in the past.

Involve family members and friends who live in another location or are unable to help in person on a regular basis. If a family member resides in another location and is unable to help in person or on a regular basis, he or she may be able to assist with online tasks such as bill payment, grocery shopping, and prescription refills. Encourage them to check in regularly with your loved one by calling him or her or sending a note or package. The below are some suggested gifts:

- A photo album with pictures of family and friends
- Picture frames
- A digital picture frame or one that has the option to record a personalized greeting

- A box of greeting cards, or stationary and stamps
- Fresh flowers or a plant (if allowed by the facility, check first)
- Scented soaps or lotions
- Homemade treats such as cookies or snack mix (check dietary restrictions)
- Holiday decorations to help personalize the room.
- Freshly baked cookies or cupcakes that are easy to share
- Framed pictures or greeting cards made by grandchildren or other family members
- A soft blanket or a pillow with a soft pillowcase
- Favorite movies on DVD (if a DVD player is available; if not, inquire about purchasing a DVD player)
- Large print books
- Audio books on CD or loaded onto an MP3 device
- A gift card to a local grocery or a retail establishment for personal items that can be used on a shopping outing
- A magazine subscription for something such as a hobby enjoyed prior to entering the nursing facility.

PREPARING FOR THE MOVE

When transitioning your loved one into an assisted living or skilled nursing facility, you will need to complete some preparation for the move. Preparation will help ensure that you are meeting all of your loved one's needs and that the transition goes as smoothly as possible for you and your entire family. It is important to consult the rules of the facility regarding what items residents may bring into the facility and what will be provided for them. A list of items to be gathered or purchased can help to guide your planning, and it is important to coordinate the move itself with all members of your family who will be involved in helping your elderly loved one move.

Here is a checklist of possible items to bring with you or make sure are available when you transition your loved one into a residential facility.

- ☐ Radio or stereo with CD player
- ☐ Mini-refrigerator
- ☐ Television (DVD/TV combinations are recommended)
- ☐ Cable or satellite television service if not provided by the facility
- ☐ A phone line in the resident room or a cell phone if appropriate

□ Headphones that are compatible with the television and radio. These headphones will allow the resident to watch TV or listen to the radio even at a loud volume or if someone else is in the room.

□ Food items that are not always available in the facility that can be kept in a resident's room, such as snacks and drinks

□ Pens and paper

□ Any needed denture supplies and containers

□ Reading glasses or other glasses if needed

□ Hearing aid if needed, and extra batteries

□ Electric razor or razors, shaving cream or gel, and aftershave lotions

□ Comb and brush

□ Makeup, body powder

□ Toothbrush, toothpaste, and mouthwash

□ Hair supplies, including shampoo and styling aids

□ Deodorant

□ Facial tissues

□ Seven pairs of undergarments

□ Disposable undergarments if needed

□ Several comfortable outfits such as sweatpants and sweatshirts or cotton T-shirts

□ Two easy-to-wash sweaters

□ Seven pairs of socks

□ Three or four pajama sets or nightgowns

□ Two pairs of comfortable shoes

□ One heavy and one light jacket

□ Slippers and a robe

□ Belts if appropriate

Using a permanent marker, make sure to mark all personal items with your loved one's name. This helps with sorting laundry and ensuring that your loved ones clothes make it back on laundry day. It is also important to provide the facility a copy of your loved one's health care power of attorney and living will documents.

Determining the best level of care for your elderly loved one in order for him or her to maintain the highest level of independence possible is no easy feat. This is a process that requires careful research, and the final decision needs to be based on the needs of the entire family. The main focus should be to ensure that your loved one is in a safe and secure environment with the best level of care available.

FIVE

Stress, Guilt, Anger, Burnout, and More: Dealing with the Impact of Eldercare on the Caregiver and the Entire Family

- Signs and symptoms of Caregiver Stress Syndrome
- Address caregiver burnout
- Help the caregiver's spouse/partner and children deal with the effects of caregiving
- Help the loved one deal with the impact

Caregivers are challenged with balancing the care of their elderly loved ones, caring for their other family members, and taking care of themselves. The physical, psychological, and emotional effects of caregiving can be considerable, even overwhelming at times, for the caregiver and the caregiver's significant other and children. Often, caregivers experience burnout that may go undetected as they focus on the care of their elderly loved ones. Other people (including the caregiver's significant other and children), and priorities (including work, hobbies, exercising, and socializing), may become subordinate to the needs of the elderly loved one. This may cause tension, resentment, anger, frustration, or confusion at home. Knowing that Caregiver Syndrome exists, as well as understanding the resources that exist to support caregivers and their families, can help you and your family deal in a healthy way with the psychological and emotional responses to caregiving.

~

A Personal Story: Carol's Perspective on Adaline's Eldercare

Carol is Adaline's sister and is 14 months older than Adaline. She has lived with Adaline in their mother's home or very close to her in the same town all their lives. Carol remembers her father telling her mother that, even as a young child, Adaline was "one to keep an eye on," as she had a tendency to get into trouble. Carol and her husband lived in their family home along with Adaline and their mother for many years while Steve and Rhonda were young children. Carol helped her elderly mother look after Steve and Rhonda while Adaline worked full time.

Adaline and Carol had an intense sibling relationship, at times disagreeing about Adaline's relationships with men and situations involving Steve and Rhonda. When Rhonda moved away to California, Adaline asked Carol to talk to her to persuade Rhonda to reconsider her move. Carol regrets trying to talk Rhonda out of moving because it strained her relationship with Rhonda, although she did it at the request of Adaline.

Carol noticed that Adaline would often say or do things in an attempt to create distance between Carol and Adaline's children. Carol, as the older sister, often felt that she came to Adaline's rescue, helping her to raise her children and providing the support Adaline needed as a single parent. She did not find Adaline particularly appreciative of her efforts to support Adaline, Steve, and Rhonda.

When Carol's mother was still alive, Carol, like Adaline, worked outside the home. Carol cared for their mother from the time she was in her late 80s until she passed away at age 100. Adaline lived with her mother throughout most of Steve and Rhonda's childhoods, and Carol believed that residence in their mother's home brought with it responsibility to assist with their mother's care. According to Carol, Adaline did not see it that way. This was an ongoing bone of contention between the two sisters—Carol recalls that Adaline seemed more interested in dating and socializing with her friends than in providing needed care for their mother. Carol also recalls arguing frequently with Adaline when Adaline appeared to place her romantic and social pursuits ahead of her children's best interests and well-being.

When Adaline was in her late 50s, she was still working at a local chemical plant as a clerical support person. Living in a small town, Carol was familiar with many of Adaline's coworkers and would sometimes hear from them that Adaline was being transferred into different work positions because she was unable to meet the expectations required of her on the job. Carol noticed that Adaline was struggling with tasks at home such as housekeeping, tracking her finances, and maintaining medical appointments. She noticed that Adaline was becoming forgetful and was frequently losing items such as her keys, her purse, and her shoes. Adaline began to rely upon Carol more frequently to function on a daily basis, with such tasks as grocery shopping, attending doctors' appointments, and overseeing her finances.

As Adaline's functional abilities declined, Carol began to notice a change in Adaline's ability to maintain the household as well as her personal hygiene and grooming habits. It was difficult for Carol to see her family homestead decline along with her sister, as she grew up in that house and remembered her mother keeping everything clean and in perfect order. Carol continued to put her feelings aside to care for Adaline as her functional abilities decreased. She communicated her concerns about Adaline's symptoms and diminishing abilities to Steve and Rhonda.

Being an elderly person herself, Carol struggled with caring for Adaline on a daily basis as time went on. This, combined with their somewhat strained relationship, made it challenging to fulfill the role of the caregiver for her younger sister day after day. Carol's husband was approaching 80 years of age, and, although he was in excellent health, it was challenging for both of them to keep up with the demands of Adaline's increasing needs.

Carol was relieved when Steve and Rhonda realized that Adaline needed more help than Carol could provide and initiated home health care assistance to monitor Adaline daily, provide her medication, and prepare her evening meal. At this time, Carol was still overseeing Adaline's financial affairs as well as her medical treatment, which combined to be an enormous responsibility. Adaline would often become frustrated with her lack of ability to perform simple tasks and lash out in anger at Carol. Carol was frustrated too, and she would sometimes become angry with Adaline, although she did not blame Adaline for her steadily progressive medical and psychological state. Given the history of Carol's relationship with Adaline and this highly stressful new situation, Carol struggled with her caregiving role, but she continued to care for her sister because she believed it was the right thing to do and because Adaline had no other family members living close by.

Perhaps not surprisingly, Carol's own health began to be affected by her caregiving role. She was diagnosed with high blood pressure for the first time in her life. She would often worry about her sister being alone at night, especially when Adaline would call wondering how to turn off the television or whether she needed to turn the furnace up. Although Carol lived only 10 minutes away from Adaline, it was becoming more challenging to be Adaline's primary caregiver and she knew she needed help.

When Steve and Kate approached Carol and presented the plan to move Adaline into an assisted living facility, she was in agreement but she was concerned that Adaline would be very difficult during the transition. Carol assisted by preparing Adaline's clothes and other items for the move to the assisted living facility and by filling Adaline's prescriptions so they were ready for the move. Carol asked that she not be there when they presented the plan to Adaline because she felt it would be received more positively if Adaline heard it from Steve and Rhonda by themselves. Carol remembered Adaline wanting to place their mother in a nursing home some years earlier, and Carol balked at the idea, suggesting instead that Adaline provide more support to their mother in the home out of gratitude for all of the support their mother had provided Adaline over the years. Carol was struck by the irony that, as Adaline came to recognize her own symptoms of dementia, she was vehemently opposed to moving into an assisted living facility even though she had wanted to place her mother in one years earlier.

Carol continues to assist Steve and his wife, Kate, in the caregiving process by watching over Adaline's home until they can sell it and checking in with her sister by phone on a daily basis. She jokes, "Some things never change," as she describes the difficulties she faces trying to reach Adaline by phone in the evening— Adaline spends most nights in her boyfriend's room! Carol's own health has improved since she has relinquished the role of primary caregiver for her sister. She enjoys being able to visit her every few months and is glad that Adaline is in a safe environment.

~

THE PHYSICAL, EMOTIONAL, AND PSYCHOLOGICAL IMPACT OF CAREGIVING

Former First Lady Rosalyn Carter said, "There are only four kinds of people in the world: those who have been caregivers, those who are currently caregivers, those who will be caregivers, and those who will need caregivers." Certainly, caregiving can be very rewarding, but it can also be challenging, even debilitating, at the same time. As a caregiver, you may feel an overwhelming sense of responsibility at times and feel helpless at other times. Each time you are with your loved one, the experience may be different based on the task being completed and the changing needs of the loved one. A caregiver may have started out just checking on his or her loved one in the home on a weekly basis and in a short period of time it could progress to daily assistance or moving the loved one in with the caregiver or to an assisted living or skilled nursing facility.

Even when a loved one has transitioned into some type of assisted living or skilled nursing facility, the caregiving does not end. In the case of Dani and Joseph, Dani started out providing caregiving tasks in her own home, and, when Joseph transitioned into a skilled nursing facility, so did the caregiving tasks, just on a different level. Dani was still overseeing all of the decisions regarding Joseph's medical care as well as his financial needs. Dani was Joseph's power of attorney for all of his medical care and veteran's benefits and his payee for his Social Security benefits.

As a caregiver, you may experience a rollercoaster of emotions throughout the eldercare process. Feelings can change from sadness to anger in a split second and include:

- Sadness
- Loneliness
- Guilt
- Denial
- Helplessness
- Resentment
- Tension
- Despair
- Hopelessness
- Stress

Caregivers may experience stress to the point of physical and emotional burnout. Caregiver burnout is common but may go undetected because the caregiver is usually juggling many responsibilities. The caregiver may not directly relate the symptoms of burnout to the tasks of caring for a loved one. When an individual makes the decision to become a loved one's primary caregiver, it is life changing. The caregiver needs to be readily available to assist at all times. And as the elderly loved one's function decreases, the caregiver will be needed more and more to provide adequate care for him or her. Although the amount of physical and emotional energy required to take care of a loved one varies for each caregiver, many experience some level of burnout over extended periods of time.

In order for the caregiver to fully commit to the needs of an elderly loved one, someone or something else becomes a lesser priority in the caregiver's life. "Something" may be work or a hobby and "someone" is most likely a close family member such as a spouse or child or both who will lose out on that quality time. This takes a toll on those family members as well. Children, spouses, and close family friends may all be impacted by the shift in responsibilities and new time commitments of the caregiver. Indeed, the caregiver often finds himself or herself "sandwiched" between layers and levels of responsibility to the people in his or her life.

Caregiving may also impact the social life of that person and the amount of time that he or she can spend doing things that would normally reduce stress. This may include spending time with friends, working at hobbies, and/or exercising. The bottom line is that the caregiver is now committing a great deal of time to his or her loved one and this means less time for others in his or her life and less personal time for himself or herself. Rearranging priorities is often a necessity to provide the quality support that the caregiver's elderly loved one needs.

Family dynamics may also contribute to caregiving stress. If you are providing care for a parent, then the family dynamics with your siblings often come into play. Emotions are usually running high when a parent is in need of care. In the best case scenario, siblings are very supportive and helpful, but often tensions and emotions erupt between siblings as they try to navigate through the needs of the loved one. Many times, the primary caregiver feels alone, unappreciated, and isolated. If siblings are far away, they may not realize the severity of the situation or how much time and effort the caregiver is devoting to the parent. This can build tension and resentment in the caregiver, who may feel like he or she has had to take over the overwhelming responsibilities of meeting the parent's needs. Siblings and other family members will react differently based on their personality, location in proximity to the loved one, ability to assist in the care, coping skills, the amount of involvement they have in the process, and how they deal with the fact that a parent is reaching the end of his or her life. Many families are able to address these needs and move forward in a positive manner. Other families may struggle.

Similarly, if you are providing care for your spouse or significant other, there may be differences in caregiving approaches from children or your loved one's siblings or other family members resulting in added stress.

The psychological, emotional, and physical impact that caregiving has on a person varies, but it needs to be monitored and addressed. The caregiver cannot adequately meet the needs of a loved one if he or she is not taking proper care of himself or herself. Released in 2003, a six-year study at Ohio State University, led by Dr. Janice Kiecolt-Glaser, found that elderly people caring for spouses with Alzheimer's disease experienced a significant deterioration in health when compared to a similar group of non-caregivers. This study also found that the caregivers had a 63 percent higher death rate than that of the control group.

Below is a checklist to identify if you, the caregiver, are experiencing signs of caregiver burnout:

☐ Disturbed sleep or unable to sleep
☐ Muscle aches and pains
☐ Frequent headaches
☐ Breaking out in rashes or hives
☐ Forgetting or putting off your own medical appointments
☐ Ignoring your own health problems or symptoms
☐ Weight loss or gain
☐ Not eating a healthy diet or exercising due to lack of time
☐ Overusing substances such as alcohol when you feel overwhelmed and/or stressed
☐ Becoming distant and losing connections with friends
☐ Feeling you have nothing positive to share
☐ Moodiness, such as sudden outbursts of anger and frustration directed at your spouse or other family members that seem to come out of nowhere
☐ Feeling sad, down, depressed or hopeless
☐ Feeling enervated
☐ Blaming your loved one for the situation
☐ Feeling that people ask more of you than they should
☐ Feeling irritated by other family members who don't help out
☐ Feeling anxious
☐ Feeling loss of control
☐ Feeling isolated

ADDRESSING AND AVOIDING CAREGIVER BURNOUT

Share your feelings. Talking about difficult and stressful situations can bring much relief. It is OK to be angry, frustrated, or even sad, and having close friends to talk to can provide volumes of support to help move past these negative feelings.

Find a local support group. If you are uncomfortable speaking to friends and family, consider a local support group through your local Area Agency on Aging, church, or county mental health department. Support groups to help cope with caregiver burnout can also be found by asking other caregivers if they know of any groups or have participated in any groups in the past. Research local chapters of disease-specific organizations, such as the Alzheimer's Association or the American Cancer Society.

Stay in touch with family and friends. Let them know that you are not avoiding them and that they are still extremely important to you but your time needs to be focused on your loved one's care. Communicating with your support system is critical during this time in your life. As the caregiver, time with your friends may focus more on quality versus quantity of time. Some of the best friends in life can go for months or even years without seeing each other and pick up right where they left off. "Sometimes friends drop you when you're a caregiver, and that's OK," says TV-radio commentator Leeza-Gibbons, founder of the Leeza's Place communities for caregivers. "Not all of them will be able to make the caregiving journey with you—but your solid friendships can still be there for you." The advantage we have with technology is that it is easy to send a quick text or email or even video chat with a friend who you may not be able to meet in person because of your caregiving role.

Involve family and friends. Invite them to assist and support you. Using other family members as well as friends to care for your elderly loved one provides you with important respite from your caregiving responsibilities. It will also help you as the primary caregiver to not feel so isolated and overwhelmed. Ask family and friends to stay with your loved one while you take care of other responsibilities or run errands.

Allocate caregiving tasks. You may be surprised that they enjoy being part of the caregiving and appreciate the fact that you are including them in these tasks. Most people who have not had any direct experience with caring for a loved one may not know how to reach out and offer help, so be specific. For example, "I need someone to come and stay the night with mom on Tuesday so I can get a good night's sleep," is more specific than "I'm tired and I need some relief." Possible tasks include:

- Completing an errand such as shopping
- Visiting on a specific day and time
- Writing checks and sending out bills
- Balancing bank accounts
- Taking out trash
- Housekeeping, including washing dishes, sweeping, and dusting
- Cleaning the refrigerator and cupboards to remove old food
- Mowing the lawn
- Doing the laundry (washing, drying, folding, and putting on hangers or in drawers)
- Preparing meals (lunch and dinner)
- Refilling prescriptions
- Transporting you to and attending medical appointments
- Transporting you to and attending church service

Even siblings, friends, or family members who live far away can provide practical help and emotional support.

Consolidate tasks whenever you can. Run all of your errands for the week in one trip. Grocery shopping or doing errands for yourself and the loved one at the same time may also save you time and energy.

Reduce your responsibilities. If your loved one has a vehicle he or she no longer uses or a home in which he or she no longer resides, selling these commodities will give you fewer things to worry about; it will allow you to focus on other priorities. Having medical oversight of your loved one by one physician can also simplify the situation by not having to communicate separately with several or many medical providers. If you can have a pharmaceutical company oversee your loved one's medications, this, too, may simplify your situation.

Make time for yourself. Because of this shift in time availability, you need to make sure that you take time for yourself and continue to do things you love to do. You should maintain as many of your former routines and customs as is feasibly possible. You are not letting your parent or grandparent down by taking some time for yourself. In order to take care of others, you must take care of yourself.

Talk to your employer. Discuss possible time off, a reduction of responsibilities, or other accommodations. Be proactive and solution-oriented. According to Jim Krosky, a Senior Professional in Human Resources, it is best to wait until you need accommodations before approaching your employer. Discussing hypothetical or possible future needs for time off might be viewed as an unnecessary burden by the employer, and it might prompt the employer to scrutinize your attendance and/or productivity more closely than usual.

Reach out to local respite care services. If you do not have anyone nearby to rely on, it is important to research local respite care services that provide a "break" from the stress and strain of caring for a loved one. Respite care service provides care for an elderly loved one for a specified period of time, allowing the caregiver to take a break or to focus on other responsibilities like immediate family or work. Respite care services include home based care, adult day care, skilled nursing, home health services, and short-term institutional-based care. Types of respite care include:

Volunteer respite care. In some areas, local church groups or the Area Agency on Aging may coordinate a formal "visitor program" in which volunteers assist with providing basic respite care services.

Adult day care services. Centers are designed to provide care and companionship for seniors who need assistance or supervision during the day. Centers are usually open during working hours and may stand alone or be located in senior centers, nursing facilities, churches or synagogues, hospitals, or schools. The staff may monitor medications, serve hot meals and snacks, perform physical or occupational therapy, and arrange social activities. They also may help to arrange transportation to and from the center itself.

At-home respite care. At-home respite care may include:

- Assistance with housekeeping tasks such as light cleaning, laundry, or preparing meals.
- Providing supervision and/or visiting with your loved one to provide company.
- Assisting with activities of daily living such as using the restroom, getting dressed, and showering or bathing.
- Providing other skilled care services including administering medicines or, if the respite care is not qualified to administer medications, assisting with opening pill bottles or pill boxes.
- Homemaker services to assist with housekeeping chores, preparing meals, or shopping.
- Assist with transporting your loved one to appointments such as to their doctors or physical/occupational therapy if appropriate.

Ways to support a primary caregiver

- Send a note of thanks and appreciation for the work they do
- Send a gift card for a cup of coffee, spa service, or restaurant meal
- Offer to do one of the caregiver's weekly tasks: picking up a prescription, grocery shopping, driving their child to school, etc.

CAREGIVER'S BILL OF RIGHTS

Although the feelings and emotions that come with caregiving may vary from day to day or even hour to hour, you do have the right to have a basic level of expectation about the caregiving. Jo Horne, author of *Caregiving: Helping an Aging Loved One*, created a Caregivers Bill of Rights that details specifics related to the caregiver role.

I have the right to take care of myself. This is not an act of selfishness. It will enable me to take better care of my loved one.

I have the right to seek help from others even though my loved one may object. I recognize the limits of my own endurance and strength.

I have the right to maintain facets of my own life that do not include the person I care for, just as I would if he or she were healthy. I know that I do everything that I reasonably can for this person, and I have the right to do some things for myself.

I have the right to get angry, be depressed, and express other difficult emotions occasionally.

I have the right to reject any attempt by my loved one (either conscious or unconscious) to manipulate me through guilt, anger, or depression.

I have the right to receive consideration, affection, forgiveness, and acceptance from my loved one for as long as I offer these qualities in return.

I have the right to take pride in what I am accomplishing and to applaud the courage it sometimes takes to meet the needs of my loved one.

I have the right to protect my individuality and my right to make a life for myself that will sustain me when my loved one no longer needs my full-time help.

I have the right to expect and demand that as new strides are made in finding resources to aid physically and mentally impaired persons in our country, similar strides will be made toward aiding and supporting caregivers.

HELPING THE PRIMARY CAREGIVER'S SIGNIFICANT OTHER DEAL WITH THE EMOTIONAL IMPACT

Just as this is a difficult time for the primary caregiver, it is also challenging for the caregiver's close family, and their feelings must also be addressed. Sometimes the primary caregiver falls into the caregiving role and the responsibilities that come with it slowly and naturally. In most cases, a parent or loved one does not have a catastrophic injury that requires instant and constant caregiving. For most caregivers, the tasks start gradually by helping with basic errands such as driving the loved one to a doctor's appointment or mowing the lawn. Frequently, the caregiving tasks increase slowly over time and it takes quite a while before the primary caregiver realizes how much he or she is truly assisting the loved one on a regular basis and the effect that has had on his or her family.

Other than the caregiver, the spouse or significant other of the caregiver may be the most affected. The spouse or significant other may also experience the physical, psychological, and emotional impact of the caregiver's additional responsibilities. Planning for the birth of a child allows a couple to have several months to prepare and begin to adjust to the life-changing event. Caring for an elderly loved one may occur quickly or without the ability to effectively plan for this transition in your relationship. Additionally, the care for an elderly loved one differs in that it is usually the parent or relative of the caregiver, and decisions made are often more emotionally charged for the caregiver. Behaviors that have been present in the parent–child relationship in the past may become more prominent during the caregiver relationship, and this may also impact the spouse or significant other. Eighty percent of caregivers in a 2009 Caring.com survey reported that caregiving strained their marriage or other relationships.

Once someone becomes a caregiver for a loved one, there is a dramatic shift in responsibilities in his or her own life. A caregiver's spouse or significant other usually takes over the responsibilities that the caregiver cannot attend to while taking care of the loved one. If there are dependent children involved regardless of the age, the spouse or significant other will now need to take over additional responsibilities such as increased oversight of children's education, extracurricular sports or activities, household chores, and finances. These additional responsibilities can cause anxiety and resentment, among other strong emotions.

The spouse or significant other may also feel resentful that his or her life has been greatly impacted while having limited input into the decision-making process because the person is the relative of his or her spouse or significant other. Raising a child together allows both parents to provide input, but this may not be the case when providing care for a parent. Some spouses of caregivers have relayed feelings of isolation during this time as they have been told that they are not part of the "immediate family" in the decision-making process. And if he or she disagrees with the caregiving situation, the stress and tension are only compounded.

Suggestions

Shift responsibilities. Instead of adding more responsibilities to your spouse or significant other, try shifting responsibilities in a way that avoids overburdening any one individual. An example of this may be having the caregiver take over paying bills or another task that he or she may be able to do while sitting with the elderly loved one and having the spouse or significant other take over carpool activities.

Maintain open communication. Many times, caregiving allows couples to communicate about very difficult topics and adverse situations, which can strengthen a relationship if done in a positive way. Share feelings, in a gentle, nonthreatening, yet realistic manner. When communicating with your spouse or significant other, always try to maintain a calm tone of voice. Many times a caregiver is feeling overwhelmed, stressed, and angry, among other feelings and emotions. Your spouse or significant other may be experiencing the same feelings, as the impact of the caregiving situation also affects him or her. It is important to appreciate your spouse or significant other and saying that is a powerful and positive way to let him or her know how you feel about the commitment to and understanding of your caregiving responsibilities.

Schedule time together. Make an effort to schedule quality time alone.

Involve your spouse or significant other in the decision-making process. Value his or her opinions, ideas, and perspective and listen to what he or she may have to say.

Identify the positive factors that result from the caregiving situation. Some caregiving couples have realized that, although caring for a parent is one of the most challenging tasks they will ever do (even more so than child rearing), this situation has strengthened their relationship by allowing them to work through adversity together. Some couples have realized that, similar to parenting, caring for an elderly loved one, though it has its challenges, can bring a couple or family together as a team in the care of the loved one. Others realize the special qualities in each other as caregivers and appreciate each other even more for those qualities.

Involve an objective mediator. To resolve certain conflicts consider involving an objective person such as a professional to assist in mediation.

~

Personal Story: Kate and Steve

The next challenge for Kate was balancing her mother-in-law's needs and emotions related to the transition to an assisted living facility with the needs of her husband and children. She was focused on making the transition as smooth as possible for everyone.

Kate wanted her children to be actively involved in Adaline's life and saw this as a new opportunity with Adaline living less than a mile away from them in the assisted living facility. She felt that the lessons her children would learn when helping to care for Adaline during this transition would be lifelong lessons. As a health care professional, Kate wanted to ensure that her children developed respect and rapport with the residents in the assisted living facility, so she encouraged them to interact with all of the residents, even those that may not appear able to communicate back.

The children enjoyed visiting with their grandmother and Kate was amazed and overjoyed at the response that her children evoked from the residents when they visited Adaline. Even the residents that appeared detached and unable to communicate would often make eye contact and communicate with her children.

Kate invited her children's friends to come to the family and community events such as Trick or Treating, the Christmas party, and the Easter Egg Hunt to allow them to enjoy the activities along with their friends. Kate was able to combine spending time with

Adaline and the family with balancing her children's social activities with their friends. She felt that teaching her children to respect and care for the elderly was an opportunity for her as a parent as well as one in which her children would be able to learn from a group of dynamic individuals with various life experiences.

Steve and Kate found that caring for Adaline was an enormous responsibility, but having her in the assisted living facility helped by having her closer to them and having the facility oversee many of the tasks that Steve was monitoring previously, such as her medication management, nutrition, and laundry, and ensuring she was seen by the on-site geriatric specialist regularly. Over the past two years, Adaline has continued to transition and her dementia is to the point that she no longer remembers that she lived in another city, often commenting that she really enjoys living in her apartment. Kate and Steve agree that while there were a few "bumps in the road," the transition to the assisted living facility went better than they ever anticipated. Kate is thankful that they have been able to focus on how the challenge of caring for Adaline has really been a blessing in allowing them to grow as a couple and work together through the challenges they have encountered. She jokes with Steve that this situation will hopefully prepare them for some of the challenges they may face as their children grow, go through adolescence, and go off to college.

Kate and Adaline have become closer than they ever had been in the previous 20 years of their relationship. Kate feels that while she and Adaline may have had their differences in the past, she is now an advocate for Adaline and needs, along with Steve, to be able to provide a voice for Adaline in her eldercare needs.

~

HELPING THE PRIMARY CAREGIVER'S CHILDREN DEAL WITH THE EMOTIONAL IMPACT

Children will not always understand why their parents need to spend so much time away to take care of their loved one. This can lead to anger, resentment, or other negative emotions being exhibited by the child. Older children may feel guilty or understand more and try to pitch in with household responsibilities, but as time goes on, they, too, may begin to feel anger and resentment as their lives are increasingly compromised by the family shifts in responsibilities. Parents should be aware of the potential of these types of emotions and make extra efforts to spend time with their children, looking at it from a quality versus quantity perspective as the caregiving tasks may be taking up so much of their time;

they should make an effort to make the child or children feel special. Each week allow the children to have quality "kid time." This time can be as simple as allowing the child or children to choose what they want to do with you for an hour each week. It could be fishing, or as simple as playing cards. In Joseph's situation, every weekend, Dani would allow each of her children one choice of quality "kid time." Sometimes it was going out for ice cream or to see a movie. Other times it was painting nails with her daughter. This allowed the children to feel special and at the same time have something to get excited about and plan for throughout the week. When Dani's daughter would feel upset about not spending much time with her, Dani would change the subject and ask her if she had picked out nail polish yet for their "spa date"; this allowed Dani to redirect the topic to a more positive one.

Combining activities may also be an option to make the children feel a part of your focus while providing caregiving to your loved one. Kate's children enjoyed being able to help with activities at Adaline's assisted living facility, such as playing Bingo and helping with coffee-social time so Kate and Steve were able to check in on Adaline while also spending quality time with their children.

Children are also affected by the caregiver's need to be focused on taking care of the elderly loved one. They may feel sad and confused at their loved one's decline and they may also feel jealous and angry as time with their parent is reduced. Each child will react differently and may not be able to express how he or she feels about the situation. It is important for us as parents to pay attention to any changes in behavior and address them immediately. Above all, children need to be reassured that they are loved and important.

Answering their questions

The amount of information you feel comfortable sharing with your child will depend on their age and maturity. Older children and teens may be ready to know basic and accurate information about the situation. With young children, it is important not to overwhelm them with too much information. Children may be close to the loved one who is in need of care and they do not always fully understand what is happening.

Common questions that children may ask include:

- When will he get better?
- Will medicine help him get better?

- Why can't things go back to the way they were before?
- Will he be able to go home soon? (For loved ones who are in a nursing facility or hospital environment)
- Can I get sick from him?
- Why does he keep asking the same questions?
- Why doesn't he know who I am anymore?
- Will he die?
- How long will he be sick?

When children ask questions such as the ones above, give them a simple, direct answer. For example, "Papa does not remember things the way he used to, so I help him with certain things," is a good response to a question about a loved one who is experiencing dementia. It is always best to reassure them that they have done nothing wrong and that, although their grandparents may be acting differently because of aging or disease, they still love their grandchildren.

Encourage children to share their feelings about the loved one and the caregiving responsibilities and how it all makes them feel. Let your children know that you understand why they are feeling anger and resentment, and find ways to allow them to work through those feelings. Journaling or expressing feelings through artwork, may also be an option.

Younger children may not comprehend the entire gravity of the situation surrounding the caregiver's responsibilities, the severity of the situation that led to the caregiving, or the unavoidable end. Based on a child's age, it would be best to share little details while reassuring them that you are making sure that the loved one is being taken care of to the best of your abilities, even though the loved one is sick and may not get better. Too much information may overload smaller children and confuse them, causing additional emotions of sadness or anger.

You can also enlist the assistance and support of the school counselor, teacher, or an external counselor who is familiar with Alzheimer's and dementia and its impact on children. Older children should be able to understand more details and sharing the information about your loved one based on their developmental level is recommended. Many have access to information on the Internet and may be searching for answers independently, so sharing proactively will allow them to have an accurate picture while getting factual information directly from you.

Involving Them

Introducing children to an assisted living or skilled nursing facility early on allows them to learn compassion, patience, and kindness in caring for others. If you want to see the impact that children have on the elderly, take them into a group of residents at an assisted living facility and watch the residents' faces glow!

Children can often look past the wheelchairs, oxygen tanks, walkers, and other assistive devices to see and interact with the elderly individual in a positive manner. One mother told a story of her four-year-old daughter who would crawl into her grandfather's bed, look him in the eye, and talk to him even though his disease would not allow him to communicate back. This mother said that she could see the twinkle in his eye when her daughter interacted with him. Not only did this interaction positively impact the elderly grandfather, but the granddaughter looked forward to her visits as well.

Involving older children and allocating responsibilities to them to be part of the caregiving team can be looked at the same ways household chores are allocated. Elementary aged children could assist by spending time with your loved one and completing activities such as playing cards or reading a book to them. Pre-teens would be able to help in folding and sorting laundry or light cleaning, such as taking out the trash, dusting, or vacuuming. Older teens could assist with cooking meals, cutting the grass, or other housekeeping tasks. If the child drives, delegate errands to him or her such as grocery shopping or other errands.

DEALING WITH GRIEF, ANGER, RESENTMENT, AND JEALOUSY

Like adults, children may experience the stages of grief during this time. They may also begin to show behaviors that they have not previously exhibited, such as crying, academic problems, aggressive behaviors, withdrawal, sleep disturbances, and longing for their elderly loved one. In these instances:

- Talk with the child about his or her feelings.
- Spend quality time together. Your child may feel neglected or jealous of the time you are now spending as a caregiver to your elderly loved one.

■ Offer your child the opportunity to express his or her feelings about the elderly loved one through journaling, writing, or expressions of art.

■ Speak to a professional counselor or your child's physician.

HELPING SECONDARY CAREGIVERS DEAL WITH THE EMOTIONAL IMPACT

Everyone involved in the care of an elderly loved one is emotionally impacted by the experience. The family member who is unable to care for the loved one due to work commitments, distance, or other reasons may experience feelings of guilt for not being able to provide a high level of support. Secondary caregivers may experience all the feelings and emotions that a primary caregiver experiences, but without the ability to provide a direct level of support for the loved one that would allow them to work through feelings of guilt. They may also feel resentful of the primary caregiver for being the one that makes all the decisions and provides the direct care. Finding a support group or talking to a counselor can also be helpful for those who are secondary caregivers so that they, too, can work through feelings of guilt or resentment.

HELPING THE LOVED ONE DEAL WITH THE EMOTIONAL IMPACT

Caregiving has an emotional impact on the elderly loved one as well. The elderly parent may resent the adult child for doing many of the tasks that the parent once did for the caregiver as a child. He or she may feel guilty or sad for being "a burden." One of the ways that this can be handled compassionately for the elderly person receiving the care is to remind him or her that he or she often cared for others and now it is time for the caregiver to return the kindness. Often, the process of one person caring for another serves to increase the bond between those two individuals.

At the same time your loved one is dealing with losing control of his or her own capabilities and life choices, he or she will often be dealing with losing many friends and relatives who are also elderly. This brings about a variety of emotions including a grieving process for his or her own lifestyle as well as for the passing of others. Allowing your loved one to express emotions is one way of allowing him or her to deal with the emotions of being cared for. It is often a fine line between allowing your loved one to express his or her emotions and keeping him or her from moving forward by focusing too much on the negative aspects of the changes that have occurred. As mentioned previously for caregivers and children involved, a support group or counselor may also be an option for your elderly loved one during this process.

Dr. Mary Dellman-Jenkins is a professor of human development at Kent State University who studies the impact of caregiving on the elderly as well as their caregivers. To help your loved one, Dellman-Jenkins suggests caregivers:

- Support their elderly loved one's emotional as well as physical well-being through the administration of his or her daily medical and other health care needs.
- Treat their elderly loved ones like the adults they are, noting that all people deserve respect and dignity at a time of life when they may feel very vulnerable, afraid, and uncertain about the future.

SIX

Alzheimer's Disease, Dementia, and Sundowner's Syndrome

- Cope with a diagnosis
- Prepare for the various stages
- Address safety, housing, communication, and memory issues
- Deal with depression, anxiety, and sexuality

Dementia is an all-inclusive term for the death of or failure in the function of the nerve cells in the brain. These breakdowns ultimately cause the lack of ability to perform even the simplest of functions such as eating, drinking, and walking, and may also impact an individual's speech, motor skills, cognitive abilities, and the ability to make sound judgments.

The most common form of dementia is Alzheimer's disease, accounting for an estimated 60 to 80 percent of dementia diagnoses. According to the Alzheimer's Organization, one in eight older Americans is diagnosed with Alzheimer's, and it is the sixth leading cause of death in America. Approximately half of all nursing home residents have Alzheimer's disease or dementia. Only about 3 percent of Americans between the ages of 65 and 74 are diagnosed with Alzheimer's, but by age 85, 47 percent have been diagnosed with the disease. The total medical cost associated with all forms of dementia in the United States in 2012 was $200 billion. More than 15 million Americans provided unpaid care for persons with Alzheimer's and dementia in 2012.

Other forms of dementia include:

- Vascular dementia, referred to as "post-stroke dementia," occuring secondary to blood vessel blockage and microscopic bleeding in the brain. Vascular dementia also impairs one's judgment and ability to plan.
- Dementia with Lewy bodies (DLB), an umbrella term for two related clinical diagnoses, dementia with Lewy bodies and Parkinson's disease dementia.
- Mixed dementia
- Parkinson's disease
- Frontotemporal lobar degeneration
- Creutzfeldt –Jakob disease
- Normal pressure hydrocephalus

The Alzheimer's Association has developed 10 warning signs and symptoms of Alzheimer's:

1. Memory loss that disrupts daily activities and an inability to remember newly acquired information.
2. Inability to make plans or solve problems especially when working with numbers or tasks that require concentration.
3. Inability to complete daily tasks such as dialing the phone or driving to a familiar location.
4. Confusion related to time and place.
5. Trouble understanding visual images and determining color or contrast.
6. New problems with words in speaking and writing, including difficulty participating in conversations.
7. Misplacing items. Frequently, in assisted living or skilled nursing facilities, residents may lose items and accuse others of stealing them, only to have the items found later in unlikely places such as a purse ending up in the shower or food turning up in the underwear drawer.
8. Poor judgment. The primary caregiver may find that his or her loved one has spent an exorbitant amount of money on a marketing scam or on grocery items that the loved one forgot were already at home.

9. Withdrawal from social situations
10. Personality and mood changes such as becoming easily frustrated, fearful or anxious. The loved one may also become suspicious of those close to him or her and show signs of depression, as well.

Consult a physician, geriatric specialist, neurologist, psychiatrist, or psychologist if you are concerned about possible symptoms you notice in your elderly loved one.

STAGES OF ALZHEIMER'S

The course and progression of Alzheimer's vary from person to person, but the disease is classified into early, middle, and late stages.

The early stage usually onsets gradually, and it is common for people to have early symptoms like memory problems, lack of interest in social activities, difficulty performing routine daily living tasks, and depression for several years before being diagnosed with Alzheimer's. Once the diagnosis is made, the person and his or her caregiver must attend to adjustmental tasks such as telling others about the diagnosis, arranging support for the impending changes in the person's life, and developing a long-term care plan.

The middle stage is characterized by ongoing changes in personality and behavior that diminish the person's ability to live independently and safely. Irritability, depression, anxiety, paranoia, sudden mood swings, verbal outbursts, aggressive behavior, increased forgetfulness, constant repetition of words or stories, getting lost or disoriented even in familiar surroundings, and difficulties making rational decisions are common symptoms of middle-stage Alzheimer's. During the middle stage, the person has difficulty and may need assistance with once-routine daily living tasks such as bathing, grooming, meal preparation, dressing, and cleaning. People in the middle stage of the disease should stop driving if they have not done so already.

During the late stage, the person usually experiences difficulty with eating, drinking, bowel and bladder functioning, and skin and body health. By this time, the person usually requires around-the-clock care because of his or her lack of ability to communicate effectively, remember friends and family, use the bathroom independently, and make sound judgments regarding his or her personal safety.

People in late-stage Alzheimer's may ask about relatives or friends who passed away many years ago, and they may exhibit irrational or violent behavior that was not part of their former personality.

TREATMENT

There is no cure for Alzheimer's disease, and treatment usually focuses on alleviating or managing the symptoms of dementia that are evident in the three stages of the illness. This is usually accomplished through a variety of prescription medications. Acetylcholine is a chemical in the brain that impacts learning and memory. Cholinesterase inhibitors increase the levels of acetylcholine in the brain and postpone the worsening of symptoms for six to twelve months in approximately 50 percent of the people who take it. Razadyne, Aricept, and Exelon are all cholinesterase inhibitors. Another pharmaceutical approach is using a drug that regulates glutamate in the brain, thereby enhancing the person's information-processing ability. Namenda is a drug that is used for this purpose. Anti-depressants, anti-anxiety medication, and anti-psychotics are frequently prescribed for people with Alzheimer's. The interactions of multiple prescription medications is a major concern for people with Alzheimer's and their caregivers, and we recommend consulting a geriatric specialist to monitor your loved one's medications.

AFTER DIAGNOSIS

Inform family and friends. Once you learn that your loved one has Alzheimer's or any other form of dementia, an immediate challenge lies in determining how to present this news to family members and friends. You may find it difficult to balance your elderly loved one's right to privacy with the genuine interest and concern that family and friends have for his or her well-being. If your loved one is able to express his or her wishes about disclosure to others within and outside the family, it is best to communicate in the manner with which he or she is most comfortable. If your elderly loved one cannot participate in the disclosure decision, it is important to be open and honest with all concerned, sharing information about your loved one's diagnosis, symptoms, and expected needs for care.

Educate yourself. Once you learn about your loved one's diagnosis, educate yourself and others about the course and symptoms of the disease. Attend educational programs with family and friends to learn more about the disease and to assure them that you would like to have them continue to be part of your loved one's life as the disease progresses. Allow yourself the opportunity to express your feelings about your loved one's diagnosis, and do the same for your family and friends. The Alzheimer's Association Caregiver Center is a good resource for information and tools available for family and friends.

Promote good physical health. Although caring for one's physical health seems like common sense in any situation, it is especially important to do so with a diagnosis of Alzheimer's or dementia. Be sure your loved one schedules regular assessments or check-ups by a doctor, takes medication as prescribed, eats a healthy diet, maintains proper hydration, exercises on a regular basis if this is possible, and minimizes alcohol intake.

Promote mental and emotional health. It's common for the diagnosed to experience the stages of grief when receiving a diagnosis of Alzheimer's or dementia. He or she may go through denial about the diagnosis; become fearful of what may happen in the future as the disease progresses; and feel lonely, frustrated, depressed, and/or angry about the situation. Safeguarding psychological and emotional health is important during this time. Ways that you can be proactive in promoting your loved one's mental and emotional health include encouraging them to:

- Join a support group
- Seek treatment from a psychiatrist, psychologist, or counselor
- Write his or her experiences in a journal to help process feelings
- Participate in activities he or she enjoys
- Maintain his or her spiritual support system
- Be involved to the extent possible in planning for the future

Complete estate, health care, and financial planning. In the early stages of Alzheimer's or dementia, have your loved one take the necessary steps to ensure that his or her wishes are carried out once he or she is no longer able to make them known.

Deal with your grief, guilt, embarrassment, and other common responses to a diagnosis. As a caregiver, dealing with grief is an ongoing process from the time you first notice signs of dementia in your loved one. Someone who was once loving, outgoing, and easygoing may become quiet, withdrawn, and aggressive. Many caregivers become devastated when their loved ones no longer recognize them.

You may also experience loneliness at the loss of your loved one's companionship due to his or her lack of ability to interact as he or she once did. Seeking support from a counselor, support group, circle of friends, or clergyperson may be helpful during this time.

Other emotions that a caregiver may experience include feeling guilty and embarrassed by a loved one's diagnosis and subsequent behaviors. Some caregivers may feel guilty about the situation their loved ones are experiencing or about having to place their loved ones in assisted living or skilled nursing facilities. They may be embarrassed to take their loved ones into public situations as their behavior may be inappropriate. Although some behaviors may seem odd or socially unacceptable, people may be more accepting once they are familiar with the situation. As long as your loved one's behaviors do not place himself or herself or others in danger, there are many activities you can arrange with proper planning. Another option is to participate in activities that are sponsored by a local support group or with others who have loved ones with the same diagnosis.

Ask for help. Do not hesitate to accept assistance and support from others. Not only does this assist you as the caregiver, it also helps other family and friends work through the process with your elderly loved one.

PRACTICAL MATTERS

Other issues that should be considered following the diagnosis of Alzheimer's or dementia are driving, communicating, memory changes and living arrangements.

Driving

If your elderly loved one is still driving at the time of the diagnosis of Alzheimer's or dementia, have a discussion with the physician about indicators of when he or she should no longer drive. A driving evaluation may be an option during this time. Have a discussion about alternative transportation options such as family members (other than the primary caregiver), friends, and your local community transportation provider. You may also need to consider whether or not your elderly loved one is able to ride public transportation unassisted.

Communicating

Communication becomes an issue with many individuals who have Alzheimer's or dementia, especially as the disease progresses. The symptoms of the disease, combined with the challenges that some elderly individuals may already be experiencing because of decreased hearing and/or vision, can severely compromise communication and, therefore, decision making.

If your loved one appears to be struggling with communication, allow him or her time to finish the thought or the sentence. Jumping in and finishing your loved one's sentences immediately will not allow him or her to effectively express his or her thoughts and feelings. Wait for your loved one to ask for help in explaining what he or she is trying to say. Repeating or rephrasing things you say also helps if he or she appears to not understand what was said in a conversation. Communicate in an environment that is conducive to your loved one being able to participate in the conversation. For example, a restaurant may not be the best place to talk as it may be loud and over stimulating.

The best approaches to communicate with your loved one who has Alzheimer's disease or dementia:

- Be aware of your speaking and slow down a little from your normal speaking pace. Do not try to speak fast; make a conscious effort to slow down and be patient in waiting for a response.
- Make sure that you have your loved one's attention. Make sure you are in front of him or her, and make eye contact if possible. Initiate the conversation by asking a question and looking directly at him or her.
- When speaking to your loved one, use short sentences with simple words. This may prevent him or her from feeling confused or anxious and enable him or her to focus on your conversation.
- As your loved one talks, repeat his or her last words in a fashion that stimulates his or her memory and helps to continue his or her train of thought. For example, if your loved one is telling a story about being on the high school football team, you may respond by saying, "What position did you play when you played football in high school?"
- Use nonaggressive questions and try not to start a question with "Why?" A person who feels defensive may experience anxiety and withdraw from the conversation.

- Use facial expressions to show that you are listening and paying attention. Smile at your loved one and nod your head, make sure that he or she is aware that you are listening.
- Encourage your loved one to talk or to continue a conversation when he or she has become frustrated after forgetting what he or she was saying to you. Strategies include slowly repeating the last part of the story and giving your loved one a warm touch while he or she is speaking.
- Be patient during silent moments. As mentioned above, do not feel like you need to jump in and finish your loved one's story or sentence. Provide more time to allow him or her to put thoughts together, and, even if the silence is awkward, make an effort to wait for him or her to continue the story or conversation with you.

Picture boards and other communication devices may also help your loved one communicate more effectively. One example of this may be a phone that allows one to place pictures of people on the keypad so that your loved one can increase communication with others by merely pushing the picture of that person to place the call. Consulting with a speech and language pathologist to obtain additional options regarding ways to allow your loved one to communicate effectively is another idea. An occupational therapist can assist with cognitive accommodations and memory enhancement strategies.

Memory Changes

As your loved one's memory changes, it is important to implement a plan of cues and mechanisms to assist you in communicating, tracking important information, and providing needed care.

- Develop a written schedule of all the activities that your loved one completes in a day and the time during which each activity takes place.
- If your loved one takes medication regularly and is still living outside of your home, it may be necessary for you to take over the medication regimen. Placing the medication in a pre-dispensed container and calling to remind him or her to take the medication is the least intrusive way you can help with this critically important task.
- Compile a list of phone numbers for your loved one if he or she is still able to use the phone. If he or she has a cellular phone, program numbers into the phone for him or her so it will be easier to call other friends and family members.

- Develop a calendar of special events such as family and friends' birthdays, anniversaries, graduations, and so on, or a card kit that has corresponding cards for each family event. For example, if a loved one has a granddaughter and a son with birthdays in the month of February, place cards in the February section of the kit that are specific to the son and granddaughter. You can tailor this kit to the specific needs of your loved one based on his or her current skill level.
- Purchase a large-faced digital/atomic clock with the time, day, and date. These clocks also come with current temperature readings. Another option is to purchase a large print calendar and mark off each day so that your loved one stays current with the year, month, and day.
- Organize the household. Labeling drawers in the kitchen with names or pictures of items in each drawer or cabinet may also assist in helping a loved one find cups, dishes, or eating utensils. Labeling closets or placing pictures on the outside to remind him or her of where shoes, coats, or other items are stored is also a helpful memory technique.

Living Arrangements

Living arrangements are based on your loved one's level of functioning and should be monitored and reviewed on a regular basis. Every person is different, but keeping your loved one in a familiar environment can often assist in avoiding additional confusion and disorientation. If your loved one is in the initial phases of Alzheimer's or dementia, he or she may be able to live independently with close supervision. Having a neighbor, friend, or other relative assist by checking in on him or her throughout the day is another way of closely monitoring the situation. Arranging a way to access your loved one's residence via a neighbor or someone who is close by enables you to check on your loved one in an emergency if you are at work or do not live close by. Your loved one needs to become comfortable calling upon others to help with tasks that he or she cannot perform independently anymore.

Safety in the home is of paramount concern. Use the Eldercare Safety Checklist in Appendix A to identify and resolve some of the most common safety issues. These include:

- Making sure that there are no loose rugs or items on the floor, including shoes and electrical cords, that may increase the risk of a fall.
- Keeping hazardous materials stored so that your loved one is unable to access them.

▨ Installing proper lighting.

▨ Applying nonslip strips to the tub or shower floor.

~

A Personal Story: Steve's Experience Related to Adaline's Safety

Safety was a major consideration for Steve in caring for his mother. Initially, he utilized a home care agency to assist Adaline with medication, meals, and daily supervision in her home. The agency's staff reviewed any safety issues with Steve on a daily basis. Steve's aunt Carol, Adaline's sister, who visited Adaline every day, also provided details regarding Adaline's safety in her home.

When Steve realized that Adaline could not be safe living on her own, he knew it was time to move her to the assisted living facility. He repeatedly found expired and spoiled food in Adaline's refrigerator, fall risks throughout her house even though he removed any risks he saw every time he visited her, and newspapers and mail stored on top of the kitchen stove. Adaline's ability to use the phone became increasingly impaired, and she was still using the stairs to go to the second floor of her home even though Steve had moved her bedroom and all needed items to the first floor.

Another indication that it was time for Steve to take over his mother's care was that she had become unable to take care of her dog. This, combined with the fall risk posed by the dog lying where she could not see it, meant that other arrangements would have to be made for the dog, but it was also emblematic of Adaline's diminished abilities to live on her own. Adaline was in the early to middle stages of vascular dementia at the time Steve relocated her to the assisted living facility in his community.

~

SUNDOWNER'S SYNDROME

Sundowner's syndrome is not a disease but a symptom of Alzheimer's or dementia. It usually occurs in the late afternoon or evening when an individual experiences symptoms of confusion, disorientation, possible agitation, paranoia, depression, and/or mood swings. Other behaviors that have been linked to Sundowner's syndrome include:

▨ Wandering

▨ Combativeness

▨ Rocking

▨ Crying

- Pacing
- Hiding items
- Aggression or acting out in anger

Individuals who are experiencing behaviors such as combativeness or aggression may be difficult to care for and manage. Many factors such as relocating your loved one, a traumatic event that occurred recently such as the loss of a significant other, or loss of function or independence may increase Sundowner's syndrome symptoms. There are many recommendations and suggestions on how to decrease these behaviors and symptoms such as:

- Utilize redirection for an individual who is exhibiting uncharacteristic behaviors such as angry outbursts or bad language to calm your loved one and divert his or her attention to something that will provide a calming effect. Redirecting your loved one while attempting to orient him or her at the same time can be challenging. Listening to your loved one and communicating directly but calmly may assist in diffusing emotionally volatile situations. Being unable to communicate one's needs or thoughts is very frustrating, so allowing your loved one time to communicate as well as offering alternative communication options such as communication aids may alleviate some of the frustration that your loved one may experience.
- Be patient with the individual who is experiencing symptoms of Sundowner's syndrome. Provide support and empathy.
- Provide light exposure for the individual in the early morning. This may help the individual set his or her internal clock. Open blinds and drapes and/or turn on a light if needed. Leaving a light on in the evening may also be helpful. Some experts recommend the use of lights that are also used for individuals with seasonal affective disorder to prevent or manage Sundowner's syndrome.
- Monitor the individual's diet and limit caffeine and sugary foods or avoid them altogether in the afternoon and evening.
- Have the individual stay active during the morning and early afternoon by exercising or other activities.
- Provide a consistent routine for the individual as much as possible. This may assist in lowering anxiety and agitation as the individual will feel more comfortable and safe with an established routine. Time schedules for when your loved one wakes up, eats meals, takes medication, and goes to bed should be followed to provide a structured and consistent schedule. Family members

should weigh the pros and cons of having a loved one participate in activities with the fact that structure and routine promote
feelings of safety and comfort. If your loved one shows signs of
Sundowner's syndrome such as increased confusion, anxiety,
or aggressive behavior when he or she is taken out of his or her
routine, this may be a sign to eliminate or reduce activities that
increase these behaviors.

- Schedule quiet themed activities for the afternoon and evening,
  such as taking a walk, watching a movie, or listening to soft music.
- Monitor pain behaviors as increased pain levels may be contributing to the Sundowner's symptoms.

  Examples of pain behaviors may include, but are not limited to:

  - Crying
  - Moaning, groaning
  - Facial grimaces
  - Wincing
  - Flushing
  - Changes in blood pressure
  - Changes in heart rate
  - Grabbing, rubbing, or touching the affected area of the body
  - Not using the affected area of the body
  - Walking or ambulating differently
  - Changes in breathing patterns
  - Changes in sleeping patterns
  - Changes in eating patterns

If your loved one is exhibiting any of these symptoms and has not
done so previously, consult with a medical provider.

- Talk to your medical provider about the potential for pharmaceutical intervention. If your loved one is depressed, his or her level of
  dementia may increase.

  Working with or providing care for an individual with Alzheimer's, dementia, or Sundowner's syndrome is a challenge, to put it
mildly. Although the preceding recommendations may help with
some of the behaviors associated with Sundowner's syndrome, each
individual will react differently. It is important to continue to try different combinations of activities and routines until you find one that
works well for your loved one.

~

A Personal Story—Dani's Experience with Joseph's Dementia

When Joseph's dementia and Alzheimer's symptoms began to increase, so did his behaviors commonly related to Sundowner's syndrome. When Joseph was living in Dani's home, he would become more anxious in the evening and would pace around the house before he became reliant on a wheelchair. This pacing would often lead to Joseph wandering away from the home. In order to be more aware of Joseph's whereabouts, Dani placed a small bell on both the front and back doors. This assisted Dani in keeping track of Joseph when she was occupied with other household tasks.

Transitioning into the skilled nursing facility seemed to increase Joseph's symptoms. Within just a few days of moving into the facility, Joseph began arguing with the staff and exhibiting anger with no provocation. Prior to the onset of his dementia, Joseph had been a mild-mannered and easygoing person, so this change in behavior came as a surprise to Dani and his other family members. Another new behavior that Joseph began to exhibit in the nursing facility was wandering into other residents' rooms and taking their personal items. On one occasion, when several missing items were found in Joseph's room, he became angry and denied taking them from his fellow residents. When Dani visited Joseph during the day, he was usually in a pleasant mood and did not ask her when he could leave the facility and return to her home, but when he called Dani in the evening he would often be sad, angry, and despondent. He would demand to know how long he had been residing in the facility and when he could move back to her home.

Dani found it challenging to answer these questions from her dad. She was always honest, but she did not want to say things that would further discourage him in his fragile emotional state. She also chose not to confront him regarding his arguments with facility staff or his theft of other residents' property. She did not want to upset him any more than he already was.

As Joseph's cognitive abilities continued to decline, he experienced an increase in symptoms related to Sundowner's syndrome. Dani began receiving more and more feedback from the facility regarding Joseph's behavior. Joseph began having altercations with his roommates, until the facility arranged for him to have a single-occupancy room. He argued more vehemently with facility staff members, threatening them with physical violence on several occasions. He also took to accusing other residents of stealing his money and personal items. Again, these behaviors were highly uncharacteristic of the kind, gentle, and affable person Joseph had been prior to the onset of his dementia.

~

LUCID PERIODS

Existing research cannot fully explain why many individuals with dementia sometimes experience lucid periods. During these periods, people with dementia, seemingly "out of the blue," revert to the characteristics of their former selves for a few minutes, a few hours, or even an entire day. During these times, you may find your loved one able to communicate clearly, to express clear memories of the past, and to think clearly and rationally about his or her circumstances.

How to Respond to Lucid Moments:

- Remain calm and treat your loved one with kindness and love the same way you would under any other circumstances. Know that lucid moments aren't triggered by anything specific, so cherish them.
- Try what is referred to as "reminiscence therapy." This is done by looking at objects or images representative of the person's past (e.g., pictures, items he or she has collected, hobbies) and create a conversation about them.
- Be patient and do not let your excitement and surprise show to your loved one. Do not try to ask too many questions or force memories.
- If possible and appropriate, play music. Some research has shown that many people with dementia will often react to music by singing or dancing.
- Do not become disappointed if your loved one is still unable to remember something specific
- Treasure these moments when they happen.

Dealing with the symptoms of Alzheimer's and dementia is complicated for all parties concerned—caregivers, family members, and elderly loved ones. Like Tom Hanks said in *Forrest Gump*, "Life is like a box of chocolates; you never know what you are going to get." This goes without saying for anyone who has experienced dementia or Alzheimer's disease from any vantage point. From moment to moment or day to day, you are not sure who is looking back at you or what he or she is thinking.

~

A Personal Story—Lucid Days with Joseph

For years, Joseph did not mention either of his daughters' names when they came to visit him in the nursing facility. He knew they were familiar and would greet them with a hug and a kiss but would never refer to them by name or how he knew them. One day when Dani was leaving the nursing facility where she had been visiting Joseph in the cafeteria, she overheard another resident ask him who she was. Joseph replied, loud and clear, "Oh, that is my daughter, Dani." Dani could not believe what she just heard, it had been so long since Joseph had made that connection out loud. Dani immediately burst into tears and contacted her sister and told her to hurry up and get to the facility because Joseph was having a lucid day. His lucidity lasted long enough for Dani's sister to spend some time with the "old" (or, if you prefer, former) Joseph. Dani and her sister called Joseph's lucid periods "good days," and they certainly were good days for these ladies who loved their dad very much and cherished their memories of the life Joseph shared with them before the onset of his dementia.

During a visit with out-of-town relatives, Joseph was having a very lucid day and reclaimed his role in the family as a friendly, sociable, and easygoing person—a charming storyteller who remembered at least one humorous anecdote involving each of his guests. Later that evening, Dani met these family members for dinner, whereupon they questioned Joseph's diagnosis and the decision to have him reside in a nursing facility. Dani tried to explain that Alzheimer's has many faces and one never knows what to expect from day to day. The out-of-town family members returned to the nursing facility the next day expecting to spend another afternoon sharing old stories with Joseph, just the way he used to be. Although he greeted them when they arrived and he employed good manners during their second visit, few traces of the former Joseph could be seen that day. Joseph's niece said it was as if he had no idea who she was and did not remember visiting with them the prior day. That may have been entirely accurate. After a short visit, Joseph politely excused himself to play bingo in the facility's activity center.

The family members were very upset, and they could not understand Joseph's radical transformation from one day to the next. Dani explained that Joseph's disease brought with it some good days and some bad days, and their visit had coincided with one of each. Dani explained more about Alzheimer's disease and its capricious course, which seemed to make the family visitors

feel better. Looking back, this story reminds Dani how important it was for her to appreciate, even treasure, Joseph's good
days—those fond memories helped sustain her during Joseph's
bad days and, subsequently, after Joseph's death.

~

In this personal story, the family members were upset by the incon-
sistencies in Joseph's responses from one day to the next. These good
and bad days need to be explained to other family and friends who
may visit with your loved one so they are not surprised during their
encounters with your loved one.

We have been discussing the perspective of the caregiver or other
close family members on the changes brought on by your loved one's
dementia or Alzheimer's disease. As we look through the eyes of our
elderly loved one, we may see that he or she is experiencing anxiety due
to the changes in his or her life. Has there been an onset of depression?
Because of their symptoms of forgetfulness or inability to remember
a whole story, many individuals with Alzheimer's or dementia may
begin to isolate themselves from others for fear others may notice these
symptoms.

Other psychological conditions that are prevalent in patients
with Alzheimer's and dementia are depression and anxiety. These
conditions are also frequently diagnosed in caregivers, as well. The
following paragraphs describe how and why depression and/or
anxiety may affect someone with Alzheimer's or dementia.

DEFINING DEPRESSION

Although everyone may experience some type of low mood or feel
down at times, this is not the same as clinical depression. Depression is
defined as a condition in which a number of feelings, such as sadness
and hopelessness, dominate a person's life and make it difficult for
him or her to cope. Some individuals with depression may also experience physical symptoms, such as loss of energy and appetite changes.
Physical symptoms of depression seem to be more common in older
people than they are in younger people. Depression is common among
people with Alzheimer's or dementia and often their caregivers, as
well. Some research indicates that depression is most commonly found
in individuals who have been diagnosed with vascular dementia or
Parkinson's dementia.

SYMPTOMS OF DEPRESSION

The symptoms of depression affect people in various ways and to different degrees.

Below are common signs of depression:

- Feelings of sadness
- Hopelessness or irritable mood for much of the time
- Increased agitation and restlessness that is out of character
- No longer interested or finding pleasure in activities that were once enjoyed
- Sudden change in eating habits
- Low self-esteem, worthlessness, or unwarranted feelings of guilt
- Feeling isolated or being cut off from other people
- Disrupted sleep or waking many times during the night
- Difficulty with remembering, concentrating, or making uncomplicated decisions
- Fatigue or loss of energy
- Onset of aches and pains that appear to have no physical cause
- Thoughts of death or suicide

Many of these symptoms of depression are similar to the symptoms commonly experienced by people with Alzheimer's or dementia. Individuals who have dual diagnoses of both dementia and depression may be struggling with even more difficulties. These individuals may find it even harder to remember things and may experience an increase in confusion and loneliness. Depression may also increase behavioral symptoms in people with dementia that may cause aggression not typical of these people, problems with sleeping, and/or refusing to eat. In the final stages of dementia, depression typically includes tearfulness, despondency, extreme fatigue, and significant weight loss.

DEFINING ANXIETY

Anxiety is an abnormal and overwhelming sense of apprehension and fear often marked by physiological signs (such as sweating, tension, and increased pulse), by doubt concerning the reality and nature of the threat, and by self-doubt about one's capacity to deal with it. Although anxiety is a normal feeling that most everyone will experience at one time or another, it needs to be taken seriously when it begins to interfere with someone's life on a daily basis.

Anxiety is the main symptom of several different conditions including generalized anxiety disorder (GAD) and panic disorder. Anxiety is known to be a common condition among individuals with dementia. GAD is a disorder that is characterized by feeling anxious about a variety of issues and situations. Individuals who have been diagnosed with GAD typically find it difficult to control their anxiety and feel anxious most of the time. Panic disorder is characterized by panic attacks. A panic attack is when the person incurs swift and unexpected attacks of intense anxiety. The attack may be accompanied by feelings of losing control and feeling as if one is going to die. Other symptoms may include physical symptoms such as trembling and sweating.

SYMPTOMS OF ANXIETY

There is significant overlap in the symptoms of the different anxiety disorders. General symptoms of anxiety include:

- Physical symptoms: fast or irregular heartbeats (palpitations), shortness of breath, excessive sweating, dry mouth, trembling, dizziness, nausea, diarrhea, stomachache, headache, insomnia, frequent urination, excessive thirst, muscle tension or pains.
- Psychological symptoms: feeling worried, tired, restless and irritable, experiencing feelings of dread and having problems concentrating

Individuals that have been diagnosed with dementia and/or Alzheimer's may also show behavioral symptoms that may include:

- Agitation
- Hoarding
- Requesting companionship at all times and expressing not wanting to be alone
- Feeling restless and uneasy
- Pacing
- Repetitive movements such as rocking or tapping fingers
- Insomnia
- Heart palpitations
- Smoking
- Biting fingernails or picking at skin
- Compulsive eating or use of alcohol

CAUSES OF DEPRESSION AND ANXIETY

Many of the things that can cause people to feel depressed may also lead to feelings of anxiety, and vice versa. The exact causes of these conditions vary from person to person, and there are often contributing factors for individuals who experience common symptoms of dementia or Alzheimer's disease.

Possible causes of depression and anxiety include:

■ Onset of a traumatic or disturbing event
■ Missing social support or experiencing social isolation
■ Mourning a loved one
■ Lack of activities, with feelings of boredom and aimlessness
■ Feeling stressed or worried over issues such as money, relationships, or the future
■ Having a past history of depression or anxiety
■ Having a genetic predisposition to depression or anxiety

It may be a challenge for a doctor to diagnose depression in people with dementia because the symptoms of depression and dementia are so similar. Unfortunately, individuals with dementia may also have difficulty expressing their feelings of anxiety to others. Because of these similarities and barriers faced by individuals with dementia, many people are misdiagnosed. The most common differences in symptoms between depression and dementia are:

■ The onset of depression commonly develops much more rapidly than dementia.
■ Difficulty with speech, reasoning, and orientation in time and space are common in people with dementia but rarely found in individuals with depression.
■ A person with depression may infrequently complain of an inability to recall things but will remember them rather quickly, whereas a person with dementia tends not to regain his or her memory.
■ Having a lack of motivation to do things can be a symptom of both dementia and depression, but an individual with depression will most likely also have an emotional reaction such as crying due to the lack of drive to do things.

Caregivers may help someone who has been diagnosed with depression or anxiety by:

- Involving him or her in exercise or some type of activity. (Dani used to encourage Joseph to run errands with her and push the cart so that she knew he was up and doing something active.)
- Encouraging him or her to talk about feelings and listening to him or her.
- Arranging activities that he or she enjoys.
- Taking him or her to visit friends or relatives.
- Providing time for him or her to spend with children.
- Involving him or her in community activities such as church, clubs, and so forth
- Bringing friends to visit.

SEXUALITY IN PEOPLE WITH ALZHEIMER'S AND DEMENTIA

Sexually inappropriate behavior is a common problem with individuals with Alzheimer's or dementia. Behaviors may vary, including lewd remarks, sexual demands, masturbating, removing clothes in public, and sexually aggressive behavior. These behaviors have been linked to individuals with Alzheimer's and dementia and are caused by the disease as the person begins to lose control and demands immediate satisfaction of instincts including sex, love, and attention. In residential facilities, sexual contact may be committed by two individuals who are both consenting to the behavior. Below are some guidelines to assist in determining an individual's ability to consent to intimacy:

- The person understands that it is his or her body and he or she has the right to refuse and that his or her body is private.
- The individual comprehends the sexual nature of the conduct.
- The person understands there are potential health risks that may be associated with the sexual act.
- The person understands there may be negative social reaction to the conduct.

Understanding the ability to consent is very complex. A detailed description is available from the Ombudsman Program for Long-Term Care. According to the Department of Health and Human Services and the Administration on Aging (AoA), Long-Term Care Ombudsmen are advocates for residents of nursing homes, board and care homes, assisted living facilities, and similar adult care facilities. They work to resolve problems of individual residents and to bring about changes at the local, state, and national levels that will improve residents' care and quality of life.

When inquiring about your elderly loved one's current sex life, some conversation-starting questions to help obtain information on what he or she may be doing and if it is a situation where you feel you may need to intervene are included below:

- Do you have a special friend?
- What do you do with your friend?
- Does this friend touch you? How? Where on your body?
- Do you touch your special friend?
- Do you like being touched this way?
- Are you having sex with your friend?
- Do you feel like you can't say no to your friend?
- Where do you have sex?
- Does this offer you privacy?
- Do you comprehend what sexual contact means?

As a caregiver, you may want to inquire if the facility where your loved one resides has an internal policy regarding residents' needs for intimate relationships and sexual activity.

As a member of the Sandwich generation, we must be aware of the emotions that may be experienced by our loved one when coping with a diagnosis of Alzheimer's or dementia. As the primary caregiver, preparing for the various stages of the progression of the disease is also recommended. One way to prepare is to ensure that safety issues have been addressed in your loved one's living environment. Housing, communication, and memory issues are also items discussed that need to be addressed when a diagnosis is made. While anxiety and depression are diagnoses that are not uncommon in elderly individuals, we also cannot forget that elderly individuals are sexual beings too, and being aware of these issues in your loved one is important as well.

SEVEN

Advocating for Your Loved One: An Eldercare Bill of Rights

■ Your loved one's rights
■ How to advocate for them

Your rights as a Sandwich generation caregiver are just as important as the rights of your elderly loved one, and it is essential that you preserve and protect your own well-being given the many people across multiple generations who rely on you for care and support. That is why we have included the Caregiver's Bill of Rights in this book. Of course, caring for your elderly loved one in the best way possible requires you to know what his or her rights are as a recipient of medical services. That is why we have created an Eldercare Bill of Rights. Though there are rights that one can find posted within an assisted living facility or skilled nursing facility, we believe there are more basic rights that one must expect as an elderly citizen, and as caregivers it may fall upon us to ensure that their rights are being met. These include:

The right to exercise independence whenever possible. Even those individuals who may not be able to make decisions without the assistance of others may still be able to participate in the decision-making process at some level. This includes the right to make decisions about his or her medical care and providers. Allow your loved one the opportunity to maintain a level of independence by doing tasks he or she is able to do with or without assistance. This may also assist with maintaining their cognitive and functional ability. Participating in treatment decisions is another way your elderly loved one may exercise his or her independence. Providing your loved one with information and the options available to him or her in the decision-making process is one way to assist in not only promoting independence but also increasing his or her awareness of the situation.

The right to be treated with respect and dignity. Your elderly loved one should be treated with compassion and care at all times by anyone who may be working with him or her to provide care or services. This includes the right to be free from harm such as physical or mental abuse or neglect. Even if your loved one may not appear to be able to comprehend information, he or she should always receive communication in a respectful and dignified manner. One way that you may be able to get a good idea about choosing a provider of medical services or a facility for your loved one is to see how the provider interacts with your elderly loved one. If the medical provider shows your loved one respect and is concerned for his or her dignity, this is a good indicator concerning the way the provider may interact in future situations. Also take note of how other elderly persons may be treated when choosing a service provider in an office setting or the environment where the services are provided.

The right to privacy and confidentiality of communications and personal information. As an advocate for your elderly loved one, educate those around you that the sharing of information should always be done in a private and compassionate manner. Confidentiality of medical information is protected under Health Insurance Portability and Accountability Act (HIPAA) rules, but nonmedical personal information should also be kept private and only shared with that individual's family members.

The right to exercise one's rights. While this may sound straightforward, many people may feel uncomfortable advocating for themselves or an elderly loved one. Knowing that you have the right to do so often prompts or permits one to do so. In many facilities for assisted living, residents will receive a written bill of rights. This may prompt them to exercise their rights if it is warranted.

The right to file a complaint or grievance when they feel their rights have been violated or a matter has been handled in an inappropriate or nonsatisfactory manner. Complaints can be filed through an ombudsperson at the organization that is receiving the complaint or grievance or through a governing body or government agency. Organizations that are committed to quality assurance standards welcome complaints in an effort to promote continuous quality improvement of their services. By filing a complaint in a formal manner, or even just offering constructive feedback for improvement, you are not only advocating for your elderly loved one but also for others that may benefit from your feedback and overall improvement in processes or services provided by that organization.

The right to nondiscrimination in the provision of services. Your elderly loved one is protected against discrimination based on race or ethnic origin, religion, age, sex, mental or physical ability, or sexual orientation. Age discrimination is sometimes referred to as "ageism" and is the act of stereotyping or discriminating against an individual or group of people due to their age.

The right to be informed of one's own status. This may pertain to medical information or information related to a resident's status in an assisted living or skilled nursing facility.

The right to live in a safe environment. While this may also seem like common sense, it is often up to the advocate/caregiver to promote and enforce this right.

As a caregiver, there are general rules of thumb that may be followed to advocate for your loved one:

Stay Informed: Keep abreast of what is going on in your loved one's life. Monitor the financial, legal, medical, and social activities of your loved one on a regular basis and intervene or redirect when necessary.

Speak Up: Don't be afraid to ask questions about medication, procedures, or any other information that may assist in the planning of your loved one's care. If you are uncomfortable in this capacity, hire someone, like a rehabilitation counselor, to do it for you.

Take Action: Don't wait for others to act when attention, services, or care is needed for your loved one.

Follow Up: Create a "diary" of any items that need to be addressed and the time frame for each. For example, if a diagnostic test has been completed, follow up with the physician to obtain the results and determine the next plan of action. Another example may be a change in your loved one's dietary needs; follow up by visiting during mealtime to ensure the new plan is being followed.

ADVOCATING FOR YOUR LOVED ONE'S MEDICAL NEEDS

If you are not a professional in the medical field, it can be quite terrifying to suddenly be making decisions regarding another person's health care and medical needs. If you have become someone's primary caregiver then you will most likely be his or her advocate when it comes to health care decisions. Caregivers need to look at themselves as part of the medical team. Even though there is already a team in place to manage and provide care from the hospitals, clinics, 24-hour surgery centers, physician offices, independent health care providers, as well as nursing facilities, you must factor yourself as the caregiver into this equation. Unfortunately as humans are providing the medical care, there is a potential for human error and medical mismanagement.

When you assume the role as an advocate for your loved one it brings a whole new set of responsibilities. Below are sensible steps you can follow to ensure that your loved one is receiving the best care possible regarding his or her medical needs and overall health:

- Any time your loved one sees any medical provider, remain involved and informed of any current treatment, change in status, or related decision making.
- Don't be afraid to ask questions about your loved one's care, medical concerns, or medication usage.
- Be prepared for medical appointments by having information available about your elderly loved one.

The following list may be helpful when preparing to advocate for your loved one at the doctor's appointments:

Medical History

- Have a well-documented history of your loved one's medical background
- Have a list and contact information for any other medical professionals that are involved with your loved one's health care
- Identify any needs for a specialist if appropriate, and discuss these with the physician
- Present medical tests such as MRIs, CT scans, x-rays, blood work, or other reports

Prescriptions

- Have a list of his or her current medications, including usage schedule as well as dosage
- Remember to obtain a prescription for refills if needed

Insurance

- Have insurance information available
- Confirm that the insurance will cover the appointment or procedure

- Have the prescription card available
- Know the benefits or requirements of ordering monthly prescriptions through a mail-in service if necessary
- Bring any medical or insurance forms that need to be completed

General

- Develop and bring a list of pertinent questions you want answered
- Schedule follow-up services or appointments following the doctor's appointment or procedure
- If you need to speak with the physician alone, contact the office prior to the appointment to avoid upsetting your loved one
- Take notes and document the information shared during the appointment. If you are not good at note taking use an "easy voice recorder" app on a smartphone or another device to record the appointment, if that is approved by the medical provider.

MEDICATIONS: PRESCRIPTION AND OVER THE COUNTER

As loved ones age or their health continues to decline it may seem like they are taking a pill for everything and anything. The most important thing you can do as an advocate is inform your loved one's medical providers of all medications that your loved one is currently taking and also the reason he or she is taking them. Do not assume that they have reviewed the chart. Even if they have reviewed the chart, all medications may not be updated. Keep an Excel spreadsheet for your loved one and bring a copy to each doctor's appointment. You can then write in any changes on a hard copy or update it electronically and resave with the current date to keep track of the most recent version. Also:

- Reiterate all allergies that your loved one has, and any reactions that he or she has had to medications.
- Inform the medical team of any over-the-counter medications or herbal regimens as well, as these may have interactions with prescription medications.

In the case of Joseph, he was on Lasix (furosemide), which is a loop diuretic (water pill) that prevents your body from absorbing too much salt, allowing the salt to instead be passed in your urine.

He was prescribed this to assist with edema (swelling) in his legs. The problem that resulted from this was that because Joseph was incontinent, the increase in urinating caused many issues with accidents or excessive changing of his adult undergarments. A few months after the swelling had gone down in both of Joseph's legs, Dani inquired about lowering his Lasix dosage. The physician took one look at Joseph's legs and opined that he could stop using the medication altogether. When Dani questioned the physician on why it was not stopped as soon as the edema had diminished, he did not give a straight answer, which led Dani to believe it was an oversight and the physician did not even realize or remember the original purpose of prescribing the diuretic. By advocating for Joseph, Dani was able to discontinue a medication that he may not have needed to be taking for quite some time.

Ask the following questions about medication:

- What symptoms are anticipated to be treated with this medicine?
- What are the most common side effects to watch for and how do I monitor them?
- Are there any other precautions such as avoiding sunlight or certain foods or drinks while on this medication?
- Is this new medicine safe when taken simultaneously with your loved one's current medications?
- Is a prescription assistance program through the drug's manufacturer available? (If your doctor doesn't know, phone the company and ask to be connected to the patient assistance program, or visit the company online. You can also search eligibility through a searchable database at Medicare.gov) Or could the physician prescribe a generic alternative or allow your loved one to be introduced to a new medication through the use of a sample packet?

Communication with one's treating physician is the key to effective medication management.

When picking up medicine from the pharmacy you will also be advocating for your loved one by addressing the following concerns:

- Confirm the medication dosage matches the physician's prescribed amount.
- Check the medication to ensure it matches the description provided.
- Clarify frequency. Is the medication to be taken twice daily? Should this be when your loved one first wakes up and at bedtime, or is it different?

- Do you have the right dosing items for the prescribed medication, such as a syringe or medication measuring cup?
- If your loved one has difficulty swallowing pills, ask about a pill crusher or splitter to make the administration more comfortable for your loved one.
- If flavoring needs to be added to a liquid medicine, will it affect dosage?

IN THE HOSPITAL

Another area in which your elderly loved one may benefit from your advocating efforts is when he or she is in a hospital environment. Many hospitals are understaffed with medical professionals who are overworked, so being there to advocate for your loved one is often necessary to ensure he or she is getting the best care. For example:

Stay with your loved one. If your loved one is elderly or has special needs many hospitals will accommodate you by allowing you or another family member to stay overnight with your loved one. The elderly may experience symptoms of Sundowner's syndrome when they are hospitalized. Even those who are not affected by Alzheimer's or dementia have been known to become confused and disoriented during a hospital stay. Being there with your loved one could help to calm your loved one's anxiety and outbursts of confusion and bring him or her back to reality.

Make every effort to have your loved one's personal physician see him or her. Many hospitals will provide a hospital generalist, who is a physician that works only at the hospital and does not usually have a private practice. While these physicians serve a purpose when needed to provide care to those admitted to the hospital, they are not usually familiar with your loved one and his or her medical history or preferences. Because of this, it may be in the best interest of your loved one to have the personal physician visit on a daily basis while he or she is in the hospital; if this is not feasible, it is then your time to be an advocate by providing detailed information and monitoring care.

Keep a record. If you are sharing the hospital duties with other family members, have a notebook you leave by the bed in which to note questions for the doctor, information for the next shift of family members coming to sit at the hospital, and your loved one's progress. Document your loved one's meal habits, or menu items he or she liked, so these can be ordered for future meals.

Ask the doctor or hospital staff if palliative or hospice care is appropriate for your elderly loved one. Palliative care is a multidisciplinary team approach to prevent suffering and pain in patients who may be at any level of disease stage.

Advocating Do's in the Hospital:

- Do attempt to choose a hospital for a procedure or scheduled surgery, then make sure that it meets your loved one's needs to increase his or her comfort level.
- Do get to know your loved one's health care team. Introduce yourself to the staff at the nursing station and always introduce yourself to any staff member that enters your loved one's room.
- Do confirm when the attending doctors will be making their rounds each day so you can coordinate and be present—this is when you will get the most updated information on your loved one's current status as well as the treatment plan. It is not feasible for any one person to be at the hospital 24 hours a day during a loved one's stay.
- Do request a family meeting with the health care team if your loved one is going to be in the hospital for an extended stay so you can be clear on the treatment goals as well as the estimated length of stay for your loved one.
- Do wash your hands and ask this of anyone who is entering your loved one's room. Even if it is a family member who swears that he or she washed his or her hands in the restroom when they entered the hospital just a few moments ago. Many other things such as elevator buttons or door handles will have been touched prior to entering your loved one's room.
- Do question the treatment if appropriate. If a staff member shows up to transport your loved one for testing, ask why if you were not aware of it. Also ask who ordered it. If you were unaware of this testing or it does not make sense to you, decline to allow your loved one to go until you can get answers to your questions. Typically, this staff member is a patient transporter and knows nothing about the testing other than the order to bring the patient to a certain department within the hospital.
- Do remember that you are the voice for your loved one. Your loved one may be weak or disorientated during the hospital stay, so you should speak for him or her and make decisions regarding his or her care.

While it is not normally recommended to go against medical advice, sometimes the rules are made to be broken. We have all had at least one experience with hospital food, and while in many facilities it has come a long way, based on diet restrictions your loved one may have, the choices are very limited. Do not be afraid to ask if your loved one can have something specific. Hospital dietary restrictions may not always be customized for each patient and are often generic restrictions such as no liquids, a mechanical soft diet, or no sugar.

It is never too early to start planning for the next step in the care of your loved one, so ask questions each day about the plan for the day related to medical tests, discharge, and the next level of care if your loved one is not going back to his or her own home or previous assisted living or skilled nursing facility. There are very specific rules related to Medicare and Medicaid coverage when one is discharged from the hospital, so be sure to work with the social worker or discharge planner at the time of admission to make sure you are fully informed on these rules and can make decisions in the best interest of your loved one. Identify one person or family member who can be a point of contact for the social worker for any discharge planning needs.

ADVOCATING FOR YOUR LOVED ONE WHERE HE OR SHE RESIDES

If your loved one is still living in his or her home you will want to ensure that it has been accident proofed based on his or her individual needs. You may need to address concerns with other family members and ask for assistance in making your loved one's home safe. When your loved one transitions into a nursing facility your role has now shifted from primary caregiver to a dual role of caregiver and advocate. You will be the main person that will notice changes in your loved one's care or behavior and you need to be prepared to advocate for him or her; in most cases he or she will be unable to do so alone.

Attend team meetings. Most nursing facilities hold monthly or bimonthly team meetings for each resident. These team meetings are made up of the Nursing Facility Administrator or Director and staff representatives from each of the following departments: Nursing, Nursing Assistants, Activities, and Physical and Occupational Therapy if appropriate. Attending these meetings is an important way to stay involved in your loved one's nursing home care and have a great audience to advocate any issues or concerns on your loved one's behalf. This also provides an opportunity to voice any concerns you may have for your loved one, or address questions you have regarding the care your loved one is receiving in the nursing facility.

In the case of Dani and Joseph, Dani was encouraged to attend these meetings when Joseph first transitioned to the nursing facility. As time went on, Dani realized that she had not been to a meeting for quite some time. When she inquired about the next upcoming meeting she was informed that through an oversight she had somehow been dropped off the invite list. So due to changes in staff or a director or administrator, Dani realized that she needed to be the one responsible for staying involved in these meetings.

Be visible. Do you know that mom who is always volunteering or helping in the office at her children's school? This mom usually has a good relationship with the teachers and staff and this can lead to a more positive experience for her children. The same school of thought goes for your loved one in the nursing facility. The more visible you are the more you will have a positive impact for your loved one. Make sure that you check in with staff while you are visiting. Drop off cookies from time to time at the nurses' station. Check in with the Activities Coordinator and inquire if you can donate a board game or another needed item that would enhance the residents' involvement and participation in activities.

Speak up and ask questions. Based on your loved one's current cognitive and/or physical limitations that led to the transition to the nursing facility, you will become the eyes and ears for your loved one. You will need to advocate for your loved one if any concerns or issues are identified. Do not be afraid to ask questions. If you notice a cut or bruise on your loved one you need to notify the staff. Never feel like you are bothering the staff with your concerns or newly identified changes in either your loved one's physical appearance or behavior. Do not assume that the nursing staff is aware of these changes. The staff sees your loved one on a daily basis and may not have noticed a change. Do not be worried that you will offend someone if you bring a concern to the staff's attention. Ask how your loved one has been recently or if there have been any significant changes. For example if your loved one usually participates in bingo daily but staff mentioned that he or she has not gone that week, something else may be going on in your loved one's life. Inquire as to how your loved one has been recently. Advocating for your loved one on a continuous basis will ensure that he or she is receiving the quality of care that is necessary for increased quality of life.

Report abuse. If you ever have a feeling that something just is not right or if your loved one expressed that a staff member treats him or her inappropriately do not hesitate to report this immediately to the nursing facility director or administrator. Action should take place immediately to address and resolve the concern. Do not worry that you will make things worse for your loved one. Any concern whatsoever regarding possible abuse needs to be taken seriously. If you feel that the nursing facility director or administrator does not resolve the issue, then take the matter to the local authorities. Any issue or concern related to elderly abuse should be handled immediately.

ADVOCATING FOR YOUR LOVED ONE'S FINANCES

If you are the power of attorney for your loved one for financial concerns, then you are responsible for making sure all bills are paid as well as for preventing fraud. Many individuals prey on the elderly in various financial scams and you will need to advocate for your loved one if you feel that he or she is being scammed or someone is taking money from him or her in an inappropriate manner. Unfortunately, this may include other family members, which makes the confrontation even more difficult, but, as the power of attorney, it is your responsibility to protect your loved one's financial well-being.

Elderly individuals are often preyed upon by individuals who have developed ways to take advantage of unsuspecting victims. There are multiple scams that target individuals that are 60 or older, including one specific scam known as the "Grandparent Scam." This scam is known to wake an elderly person in the middle of the night with a young person claiming to be his or her grandson needing money due to a desperate situation such as being in a car accident, in jail, or in another country. The person claiming to be the grandson will likely say not to tell his parents about his situation but asks that the grandparent wire money to him immediately. The grandparent is usually caught off guard and startled by the call and may wire the money to the number provided. Other scams include people posing as telemarketers to ask for donations for local or civic causes or posing as a representative from a large retail chain saying that the elderly person has won a sweepstake but they need to pay taxes on the prize in order to claim it. Another scam that has been known to target the elderly is when an imposter poses as someone from a government agency convincing the elderly person that they need to pay fees for products or services based on new government regulations.

Advocating for your elderly loved one includes educating yourself and your loved one of ways to safeguard his or her identity and finances from con artists. Ways to increase protection from scams include:

- Obtain detailed information from the caller to confirm the emergency situation or need for fees.
- Use common sense and question the caller about details that would confirm who the caller may be, such as date of birth or other specific identifying information.
- Don't act or respond in a panic mode.
- Protect the personal information on your computer or other devices to avoid con artists accessing this information.
- Never wire or send money to someone you do not know.
- Contact your local law enforcement agency to inform them of the contact.
- Check the Federal Trade Commission's website at www.ftc.gov for the latest scam alerts.

ADVOCATING FOR YOUR LOVED ONE'S END-OF-LIFE ISSUES

Having all of your loved one's wishes documented as discussed in Chapter 3 will allow the power of attorney to be prepared and able to make the difficult decisions for your loved one. This will also assist in defusing any family animosity regarding the decisions. A sibling may announce that your loved one wanted to be buried in the state where they were born when no one else had ever heard this request. Sadly, you may have other family members who are more focused on chipping away at their inheritance and are demanding a no-frills funeral and cremation versus the plans for a burial that your loved one requested. You again will find yourself advocating for your loved one's wishes and any documentation that you have to support these wishes will make this process as uncomplicated as possible.

~

A Personal Story: Dani's Experience Advocating for Joseph

When Joseph became a permanent resident in a skilled nursing facility, Dani's role now included ensuring his needs were being met as well as overseeing all decisions for him. Dani realized very early on that even though Joseph was now receiving care in a skilled nursing facility, she would still play an important part in his life as his advocate.

The first time Dani found herself advocating for Joseph was in regard to an on-site bank account. Joseph was allowed to open up an internal banking account at the skilled nursing facility. Dani would deposit a certain amount of money each month as Joseph did not leave the facility unless it was planned well in advance, but he liked to have a little money to purchase items from on-site vending machines. During the first few months, Joseph would call within a week of the deposit requesting more money. Dani was unable to determine where the money was going but withdrawal statements confirmed that Joseph was taking out as much as $20 each day. Dani intervened and put a daily maximum on Joseph's withdrawals so that he could still have money to spend on items in the vending machine and feel like he was able to make those decisions independently, but at the same time he would not be losing excessive amounts of money or at risk of being taken advantage of by others.

Dani advocated for Joseph on other occasions during his stay at the skilled nursing facility that included formally blocking a family member from calling or visiting him. This family member had issues with the fact that Dani was overseeing all of Joseph's affairs including his finances. Dani found out, unfortunately too late, that this family member was showing up or calling Joseph to express dissatisfaction in the caregiver responsibilities as well as power of attorney assignment. Because of Joseph's dementia, these experiences were both confusing and upsetting him tremendously, and it resulted in him refusing to eat. Dani was informed of Joseph's refusal to eat and she or her sister would either call or go to the nursing facility to encourage him to eat something, which sometimes would be as little as a few slices of a tomato. This lack of nutrition eventually led to an extremely low potassium level that caused him to have a heart attack and be hospitalized for several days. Dani spoke on Joseph's behalf to the nursing facility staff and directed them to not accept calls from this family member or allow him on-site for visitation.

The nursing facility was very supportive, and Dani felt that her involvement and visibility at the facility assisted with the staff's support to meet this request.

~

Advocating is an important part of the caregiver role. It is critical to the overall care and well-being of your loved one.

EIGHT

Pulling it All Together:
10 Essential Strategies
for Caregivers

Caregiving is a challenging task when caring for one individual, but being part of the Sandwich generation caring for elderly loved ones as well as our children is an even greater challenge. This, combined with the increase in Alzheimer's and dementia among the elderly, places many of us into a large pool of people caring for our loved ones. Throughout this book, we've provided a large amount of information and tools to help you develop a comprehensive and individualized eldercare strategy. Everyone's situation is unique, but the 10 strategies outlined in this chapter will help every caregiver as they try to care for an elderly loved one while also raising children.

1. REALIZE YOU ARE NOT ALONE

While it may seem as if at times you are the only person in your position and the weight of the world is on your shoulders, the more than 77 million Baby Boomers born between 1946 and 1964 have created a need that transitions many of their children into the caregiver role. This, combined with the increase of individuals with Alzheimer's and dementia in the United States—affecting people's memory, reasoning, language skills, physical functioning, personality, and interpersonal interactions—explains an increase in many of us providing care and treatment to our elderly loved ones with these symptoms. Not only are we seeing a rise in the diagnoses of the aforementioned diseases, but also an increase in medical advances that allows longer life expectancies than ever before. While it may appear a daunting task to care for so many folks who are among our country's national treasures, it is good to remember that many elderly individuals work well into their 70s and 80s.

Given the magnitude of the sheer number of individuals mentioned above, being a caregiver automatically puts you into a very large pool of people. Have you ever talked to another person and found that they were in a very similar situation to yours? This shared situation may have been a positive one or one that was very challenging, but the mere knowledge that you shared this commonality with another person may have made you feel better about the situation.

Knowing that you are not alone also helps when you can tap into the experience of those who have been in your situation, and you can benefit from that experience. Don't hesitate to ask for help or information from those who have gone before you in the role of caregiver. Joining support groups is one way to tap into someone else's experience. Ask your physician or other health care provider about other resources to support you.

Not only does talking to others who have been or are in the same situation as you assist in the process of knowing you are not alone, but it also allows you to gather information based on other people's experiences in an effort to make informed decisions about the care of your elderly loved one. While talking with others is recommended, it is also good to remember that everyone's specific experience and situation still differ, and making a decision based solely on someone else's situation is not recommended.

As you are traveling this path with your loved one, you are also not alone in this situation. Your loved one's participation is very different compared to yours as the caregiver, but you are still in this journey together. Most people are so busy and spreading themselves so thin to meet the obligations of their lives and their children's lives, in addition to their elderly loved ones in need of care, that they do not realize that this situation encompasses such a large group of people that it has been labeled with its own name. So, while we are regularly sandwiched between caring for our children and our elderly loved ones, we are not alone in this role.

2. DEVELOP AN ATTITUDE OF GRATITUDE

While this may sound a bit "Pollyanna" like, this may be just what you need to get through the toughest days while you are caring for both your children and your elderly loved one. Keep a journal of the positive things that occur on a day-to-day basis. Dr. Norman Vincent

Peale wrote many books on the power of positive thinking that focus on rising above problems and visualizing solutions to surmount them.

The old adage, "out of the mouths of babes," means that children often say insightful or remarkable things. It is sometimes the things that children may say that put things into perspective. It is often through the observation of children that we can begin to appreciate the simpler things in life. One way to identify things to be appreciative of in life is to look at life through the eyes of a child. Try it, and see if you become more appreciative of the little things in life.

One caregiver listed the following items of gratitude related to the caregiving process.

I am grateful for:

1. Being able to care for my elderly loved one (even though it is the most challenging thing I have ever done).
2. Having an excellent medical team to support me and my loved one.
3. Having a supportive spouse and family to help me.
4. Having an uninterrupted cup of coffee.
5. Those who provided care before me and have been willing to share their wisdom.
6. Seeing my children learn to be compassionate for others through this process.
7. DVR, which allows me to see my favorite show when everyone is asleep.
8. The flexibility in my work schedule that allows me to be the primary caregiver to my mother.
9. The experience of this process, which can help to make it smooth for my children when they may be in this situation.
10. "Chef on Demand" services from my local grocery store.
11. Online bill payment and banking.
12. The ability go to my "happy place" when I play my guitar.

While we have discussed how stressful it may be to be the primary caregiver and the impact on family relationships, some caregivers have shared that the process of caring for their elderly loved one actually allowed them to become closer with a sibling. We have also mentioned previously that Kate and Steve felt the caregiving process strengthened their relationship, and this too may be an attitude of gratitude for some couples. Though on some days it may seem next to impossible, finding your attitude of gratitude may be just what is needed to be able to see a glimmer of hope in a very challenging day.

While it may not be something that is first and foremost in your mind, your caregiving and the positive and negative aspects that come with it are being observed by your children. It is important to remind yourself of this, as you are role modeling this behavior for your children and this may be a life lesson to teach them about caring and compassion. As such, one might argue that this too can be an attitude of gratitude.

Another aspect that one caregiver identified as an attitude of gratitude was the social opportunities, activities, and friendships that his elderly loved one developed as the result of moving into an assisted living facility. He said he was fearful of his mother being lonely and isolated once she moved into an assisted living facility, but the truth of the matter was that she was more socially active than she had been in years with all the parties, sing-alongs, and outings available to her. She developed new friendships and was "dating" as she had not done for many years when she lived at home alone. He was so grateful that she said she was happier than she had ever been in her life after he had prepared for the worst related to her being unhappy when he moved her from her home.

Watching a comedy movie or even taking a few minutes to watch some comedy clips on the Internet may help to lighten the load. Laughter has been the focus of many studies that reveal a healing effect when people are ill, and an added bonus is that it also burns calories. Remember to laugh and identify things, situations, or actions that make you feel grateful for what you have, and focus on them on the days that you are struggling to balance the role of caregiver. This can become your "attitude of gratitude" and will help you through the days that are most challenging.

In the case of Joseph and Dani, Dani would often find humor or something that made her happy in the smallest of things or events. Her sister would just shake her head at her and ask how she did it. Dani would always say that there was so much in life that was hard and overwhelming at times that you sometimes need to create your own little happy moments. It could be something as simple as going out for ice cream at 10:00 o'clock at night or getting a pedicure. These small moments will help you rejuvenate and reenergize when you are focusing so much of your energy and emotions on your loved one.

Here is Adaline's personal story of her eldercare process and attitude of gratitude that has helped her transition into the assisted living facility.

~

A Personal Story: Adaline's Own Story

Adaline began to notice her loss of memory when she was in her mid-50s. At the time she was working full time and helping to care for her mother, so she attributed it to being overworked and stressed. She would often feel as if the world was "spinning too fast" and that she could not keep up with other people or events. She got to a point where often worked on weekends, as she was unable to keep up with the demands of her job and was not able to learn new tasks such as working on a computer. Adaline enjoyed taking pictures, and one year, for Christmas, her children bought her a new camera with corresponding printer that allowed for printing off pictures directly by placing the camera on the printer. Although Adaline was grateful for this gift, she was unable to understand how to set it up, let alone use it. She found technology becoming more challenging and a barrier to her being able to accomplish tasks.

She would often share her frustrations with her daughter Rhonda, who would provide recommendations and tools for her to adapt to the situation. Adaline found that she was unable to effectively use the tools, including a daily planning calendar, due to her symptoms. Adaline had a dog that had multiple medical needs and she began to collect a shoebox full of medications prescribed by the veterinarian for the dog. Adaline was unable to understand how to dispense the medication or follow the dosing instructions. As she approached 70 years old, she began to have more difficulty driving and would have incidents with small accidents. She noticed that her passenger-side mirror was broken off; she told her son that a rock flew up and hit it, although she thought she may have run into a mailbox and knocked it off.

Adaline realized the decision to allow the man from the bar to move in with her was not a good one shortly after it occurred, but she was glad to have someone living with her even if she was providing financial and other support to him. On several occasions when Steve said he was going to remove the man from her home, prior to the phone incident when Steve heard the man yelling at his mother, Adaline begged him not to do so. Adaline always had an eye for men, and in this case, she also felt that it was comforting to have someone else in the house with her. She knew that she had something wrong with her, but she continued to try to compensate with her children as she was fearful of what they might do with her if they knew the full extent of her symptoms.

Although Adaline was apprehensive, she agreed to go along with the visit by the Area Agency on Aging's social worker as well as the comfort care company. She struggled with having someone in her home to help her and complained that they would often do too much for her. While she realized that the things they did such as cleaning or preparing meals were things she could no longer do, she would often complain to her children to make them think she was still able to function independently in these areas. She became frustrated with all of the simple things she could no longer do, such as dressing, bathing, and grooming herself. She wanted her friends and family to know that she was still independent and could make her own decisions. It was frightening for her to think of what might happen to her if her family knew of all of her deficits.

Adaline had continually told her son that she did not want to be in a nursing home. She also became very overwhelmed when she visited him and his family bacuse she felt that she could not keep up with activities or events. One time Steve and Kate's close friends unfortunately had to close their business, and Steve and Kate took Adaline with them to visit them during this difficult time. Adaline had known these friends for over 10 years so she was familiar with them, but she was confused about what was going on and became angry and combative at their friend's business location. Adaline knew she was acting like a child but felt left out because she could not understand what they were talking about and why everyone was so upset. She wanted to be included in the discussion but was too confused by what was being said to be able to understand what was going on.

She became embarrassed when she did things that revealed her memory deficits, such as preparing her meal twice during a visit to Steve and Kate's house. What made it even more difficult was that Kate's mom also observed this event, as Adaline and she were the same age and Adaline saw Kate's mom continue to be independent and live a full life while she felt she was losing her own life and independence.

When Steve and Kate presented the option of living in an assisted living facility, they did so by calling it a retirement apartment. This made Adaline feel better as it sounded more independent to her. She was glad that she was able to be so close to them and her grandchildren. While she realized she had some challenges in remembering things during the transition, she was glad to have Steve and the family stay with her for the first week to be able to feel more comfortable having familiar faces around in this new environment.

Adaline realizes that she is in a safe place and that while she forgets how often she is visited by Steve and his family, she has a feeling that they are close by at all times. Every time she visits them at their house, she comments on how close it is to her home. She talks about the assisted living facility in a way that leads one to believe she feels at home as she says she hasn't been able to mow the grass or clean the house when referring to her room at the assisted living facility.

She admits she is happier than she has ever been in her life. Kate asked her recently what she thought of her residence in the assisted living facility, and Adaline responded that she had "nothing to complain about." She said that she had a large network of friends who stick together. She also said she enjoys all the activities provided by the facility.

Kate often teases her that it is because she has her pick of men in the assisted living facility and she can visit or "go out" with a different man every night. Adaline finds this amusing as she isn't shy about her love of men. Even when Adaline struggled with having to begin to use disposable undergarments due to incontinence issues, Kate used this as an opportunity to add humor by telling her that she would not have to go "commando" anymore if she had an accident. Adaline found this amusing as well, and they both laughed at the situation that could have been embarrassing for Adaline.

Adaline enjoys all the activity they provide at the assisted living facility, as well as seeing her family regularly and being involved in her grandchildren's lives. She is comforted knowing that Steve oversees all of her needs and she doesn't have to worry about anything related to finances, medical care, or daily activities. She is relaxed knowing that she is in a safe environment with family close by.

~

3. RECOGNIZE THAT YOU ARE ONLY HUMAN

It's a bird, it's a plane, it's . . . an unbelievably capable, talented, and caring HUMAN being. Yes, as the caregiver you are an incredible individual who may feel like you are "leaping tall buildings in a single bound" every day, all day, when you are in the Sandwich generation. OK, so maybe you don't have x-ray vision, the ability to exhale with hurricane force, or freeze objects with your breath. However, some days you may feel invulnerable or as if you have superhuman strength based on all the tasks you accomplish taking care of your loved ones.

One family member shared a story that when confronted with a particularly difficult task or day ahead, she would joke with a friend that she would "put on her cape" and get the job done. Miraculously, she was always able to pull off the challenge presented to her, though this was not without blood, sweat, and tears on some days and a feeling of complete exhaustion on others. For Christmas one year, her friend bought her a superhero costume as a joke. While this may sound funny, it is good to put things into perspective and realize that sometimes we set the bar too high and may even occasionally set ourselves up to fail. Recognizing that we are, after all, only human, and cannot perform superhero feats (at least, not every day) can put things into perspective and allow us the opportunity to prioritize what needs to be done on a daily, weekly, and monthly basis.

Literally or figuratively (whichever works best for you), try putting your cape on one day and see how it feels to recognize that you do have some superhuman qualities as a caregiver in the Sandwich generation and that some days rival those of Superman. If nothing else, you may get a good chuckle when you look in the mirror!

4. SET REALISTIC EXPECTATIONS

Are there days that you feel like a circus high-wire act, always in careful balance so as not to fall? Many caregivers are in the situation of balancing the needs of their children, spouses, parents, and work, all while trying to enjoy life on occasion.

As caregivers, many of us may have tendencies to try to meet the demands of everyone in our lives. On a daily basis, we are asked to provide support for school, work, church, or other groups. But as a caregiver, it is best to set realistic expectations for yourself and be fully informed what is expected of us up front—prior to taking on any additional roles.

You may have volunteered for something that was presented to you in one way, only to find the expectations were much greater than those that had been presented to you. A caregiving colleague relayed a story of how she was asked to be part of an executive committee for a local charity and was told that there were minimal requirements, mainly a monthly meeting and some meeting preparation. When she agreed to take the position, she found the expectations to be much more involved than what was verbally relayed to her. Obtain the requirements of a job, task, or activity in writing whenever possible to make a fully informed decision and to be able to determine if you are able to meet the demands of the situation.

If your desire is to participate in activities to support a group such as the Parent Teacher Organization (PTO), find activities that allow you to provide support on an "as needed" basis. For example, if you want to be involved but cannot do so on a consistent basis such as helping the teacher in the classroom each week or committing to the monthly "teacher appreciation" luncheon, sign up for the general help or overflow list so that you can be contacted when they have a special need on an occasional basis. You can also let your organization's leader know that you would be interested in helping out, but your situation does not permit you to do so on a regularly scheduled basis—ask them to let you know when something comes up that you might be able to help with as a one-time option.

Having a spotless home may be your preference, but is it your priority? As caregivers, most of us can find that list of items that we always aspire to accomplish around the house. The question we may ask ourselves is, are they really priorities for us given all our other responsibilities? Some caregivers have said that most days it is an accomplishment just getting the kids out the door in the morning or even getting themselves dressed.

Placing our priorities in order of what is *needed* versus what is *wanted* or preferred is a helpful tool to be able to "walk away" from or "table" some of those tasks that are not a priority. Below is a sample list developed by a caregiver of items or tasks that she needed to manage and how often versus those that she preferred to have completed.

TASK	FREQUENCY	PRIORITY
Pack Kids' Lunches	Daily	Needed
Clean Out Fridge	Monthly	Wanted/Preferred
Change Car Oil	Quarterly	Needed
Organize Grandma's Closet	Monthly	Wanted/Preferred
Sweep Out the Car	Monthly	Wanted/Preferred
Pick up Prescription	Monthly	Needed
Grocery Shopping	Weekly	Needed
Write Checks/Pay Bills	Weekly	Needed
Cut the Grass	Weekly	Needed
Clean Windows	Monthly	Wanted/preferred
Call Brother in Dallas	Weekly	Needed
Attend PTO Meeting	Monthly	Wanted/Preferred
Attend Church Service	Weekly	Needed
Bubble Bath for Me	Weekly	Needed
Kid's Dentist Appointment	Biannually	Needed
Attend Retirement Dinner of an Acquaintance	One Time	Wanted/Preferred

While developing a list may be time consuming, it allows you to place items in order of your priority and also provides a visual to do so. One might argue that taking a bubble bath or attending a church service weekly may not be a priority, but this exercise allows each individual to tailor the list to his or her needs. It also helps in looking at your daily, weekly, or monthly obligations to determine if their frequency may be able to be altered. For example, is it possible to complete the bill writing function on a monthly or biweekly timeline versus doing it weekly? Can you cut the grass every 10 days, or during a rainy spell does it need to be cut every five days? One caregiver said she made lunches for two days at a time to be able to save time for other priorities.

Another example listed above is attending the dinner of someone who is an acquaintance to you. Seeing this in writing may assist in determining the level of priority you would give to this event as compared to the person being your coworker of 15 years who is retiring. You can even take this list one step further and list your priority items in the order of 1, 2, and 3 to help you determine the rank of each task.

5. K.I.S.S.

Keep It Simple . . . Successfully! Most of us have heard of the K.I.S.S. principle in design, where keeping it simple is a goal in avoiding unnecessary complications or complexities. While the last "S," for our purposes, focuses on how we can be successful in this approach, this principle can be used in leading us to implement techniques and strategies that can simplify our lives as caregivers in the Sandwich generation. Focusing on simplicity in life is one way to "declutter" our lives as caregivers. Implement strategies and techniques to simplify your role as a caregiver.

Don't be afraid to ask for help to simplify your role as a caregiver. For example, if your loved one is eligible for a disabled parking permit, this may be one way to simplify your life by allowing them to participate in activities that you can provide easier access to by taking advantage of disabled permit parking.

Media is often provided in large print, so if this is a need for your elderly loved one, ask about it at church, your favorite restaurant, or regarding a newsletter that you receive to see if this is an option. Another way to simplify your life may be to have your loved one begin to use a motorized scooter or even a wheelchair with a grocery basket in the front. This may afford both you and your loved one some additional independence while shopping that you may not have otherwise.

A caregiver shared a tip that her mother-in-law implemented when it became challenging for her to handle glasses or large cups in restaurants due to her arthritis. She said that she would ask for a styrofoam, plastic, or paper cup with a lid, so if she accidentally knocked her beverage over there was a minimal spill and less stress.

Another caregiver said that her mother became frustrated when eating meals as she was often unable to maneuver the utensils to feed herself. This was especially true when they were eating at a restaurant or in public. In an effort to decrease her mother's frustration, she would order food that was easier to eat and that her mother really enjoyed but did not often get in the assisted living facility, such as grilled cheese sandwiches or finger foods like fried shrimp or wings. Pizza was another option that, if cut into small slices, allowed her mother to consume it more easily. She also found that her mother preferred to eat foods on the kids' menus at many restaurants and that most proprietors would allow them to order from this menu for her elderly mother. This option not only allowed her mother to eat foods that she liked and did not get often, but also allowed her to have food that was easier for her to eat. The bonus was that the kids' meals were usually very cost effective as well.

Another example of simplifying daily tasks was conveyed to us by a caregiver of a woman who had dementia. In the initial phases of caring for her mother-in-law, she would always bring along her purse, as her mother-in-law would always have that purse with her prior to the onset of her disease. As her disease progressed, the mother-in-law would forget her purse, and it became the responsibility of the son or daughter-in-law to carry it and make sure it was not left behind. A remedy to this situation was to include any of the items that she needed such as tissues, lipstick, and her identification card in the daughter-in-law's purse instead of having to carry around both purses. While this may seem very simplistic, we often get into habits of doing things one way and may not think to explore alternate options.

6. USE AVAILABLE RESOURCES

While you may feel like you are the only person in the world doing what you are doing in the role of the caregiver, the reality is that there are many of us functioning in this role in the Sandwich generation.

As we mentioned previously, you are not alone in your caregiver role. The beauty of this is that with a little coordination, you may be able to pool your resources and join forces with another person in a similar situation. One way that you may be able to do this is by supporting each other in daily meal preparations. If each one of you makes a double batch for a dinner one night a week and shares with the other, there's one night's dinner that is already made for you.

If you can combine your resources and create an adult day care group for a few hours each week, where you can come together with other caregivers and your elderly loved ones, this is a way to get needed support from others in the same situation. You may also be able to rotate if you have enough people in the group to allow one or two of you to take a couple hours away while your elderly loved ones participate in the group. It is important to make sure that your loved one is in a safe environment and with another competent individual who can provide appropriate care in your absence.

If your loved one has the ability to help you with tasks such as cutting coupons, placing return address stamps on envelopes, folding clothes, or other household tasks, allow them to do so not only to help you, but to also to allow them to contribute and feel good about accomplishing something. One family shared that the first Christmas that she moved her loved one into an assisted living facility, she had a project that required stuffing candy into containers and the residents all assisted in this project. They all appeared very appreciative of being able to contribute to the project, as evidenced by their willingness to continue to do more work even after all of the candy was placed into the containers. They also enjoyed "sneaking" a few pieces as they completed their task.

Having your elderly loved one provide assistance to your children can also be a resource for you as the caregiver. An example of this may be when a child is required to read to an adult for a school assignment. This is a good way for your child to practice their reading skills while also involving your elderly loved one in the task. While as a society we are moving toward electronic media even within the schools, if you are the parent of an elementary school student you may still be inundated with multiple paper assignments coming home on a daily basis. Children often take pride in their work and may not want it to be immediately filed or thrown away. Children can share their work with the elderly loved one by explaining the assignment to him or her. This not only allows the child to share his or her work, but also to review the educational content with the elderly loved one.

Church confirmation classes, boy scouts, or other youth-oriented organizations within a local high school or school system require a certain amount of community service hours be completed by an individual. Call upon these groups as resources to assist you in your needs while you are giving care for your elderly loved one. These individuals may be able to assist you with tasks around the house or even sitting with your elderly loved one while you attend to another task in another part of the house or outside.

As your children get older, they too can become a great resource in helping you accomplish the tasks you need to do regularly. A friend said that she recently began to have her nine-year-old daughter help her with the bill payment process. Initially, she introduced her daughter to the process by having her put a stamp and return address on the envelope. She then began to have her daughter review her check to make sure it matched the bill or invoice. Finally, she had her daughter begin to write the checks and she would then review and sign the checks, place the bills and checks in their envelopes, and have her daughter take them to the mailbox. If your elderly loved one is able, these are items they may be able to help with as well, and these tasks will provide a cognitive exercise for them as well as a teaching tool for your children.

You may find that your "resources" may be nontraditional and creative ways to allow you to care for your elderly loved one in a way that maintains a level of calm whenever possible. An example that a caregiver provided to us during an interview was that her 93-year-old father with dementia was staying with her for eight days while her 73-year-old mother, the primary caregiver, took a much needed vacation. Though her father was able to be redirected during the day when asking questions about where his wife was, he became inconsolable at night and constantly paced between the bedroom and bathroom while asking his daughter where his wife was. She would tell him and he would go back to bed for a few minutes until he forgot and came back out of the bedroom to ask again where his wife was. This kept him as well as his daughter and her husband up most of the night. The daughter realized that as he was in bed, he would wake up and see that his wife was not next to him and come out and ask about her. So she decided to try something creative. She placed one of her daughter's dolls with the same color hair as her mother in the bed next to him with the face facing away from him. She also put a large body pillow beneath the blankets so it looked as if there was a person in bed next to him. After three nights of no one getting much sleep, this appeared to work in allowing him to think his wife was next to him when he awoke in the middle of the night.

While this may seem a very unique way to address the problem, it worked, and everyone felt much better after a decent night's sleep. This is one example of how a caregiver may need to "tap into" his or her creative thought process to come up with solutions to challenges that may occur in the process of providing care to an elderly loved one.

Another area in which you may be able to access resources in is the workplace. Jim Krosky, a senior professional in human resources (SPHR), recommends that employees utilize the following resources in the work place:

- Use pretax benefits offered by your employer such, as dependent care, flexible spending, or the Employee Assistance Program for counseling or developing legal documents such as a will or power of attorney, if needed.
- Ask your employer if a benefit broker is available to provide education so you have an understanding of every benefit in the plan as an employee.

7. ACCEPT THE THINGS YOU CANNOT CHANGE

The Serenity Prayer is the common name for an originally untitled prayer by 20th century American theologian, Reinhold Niebuhr. The prayer has been adopted by various 12-step programs and can be found in multiple media contexts and publications, but it is also relevant here.

The best-known adaptation is:

God, grant me the serenity to accept the things I cannot change,
The courage to change the things I can,
And the wisdom to know the difference.

As you go through the journey of caregiving and watching the decline of your loved one, to maintain your own serenity you have to accept the things you cannot change. For example, Dani wished constantly that Joseph would recognize her and felt sadness every time she visited him in the nursing facility. She could tell that he knew she belonged to him somehow by how he would hug her hello and ask for things such as a new coat or his favorite chocolates, but he had not said her name for years. Another oddity in his dementia was that he always knew his grandchildren and would even ask Dani when she was bringing them to visit, yet he did not make the connection that she was his daughter. Dani realized that her sadness was not going to bring Joseph's memory back, and she needed to accept this fact and move on for her own sanity. When you face a difficult challenge or situation common to providing caregiver tasks, it is often in your best interest to take it in stride and maintain flexibility whenever possible.

On another occasion, when Joseph was in the ICU following a heart attack, he began to make up very outrageous stories. He would tell Dani that he was in the Korean War and had spent months in a foxhole. Dani kept trying to redirect Joseph as he would tell the story over and over—as soon as he would finish, it was as if he was on replay and he would start the story over again. Dani was concerned that Joseph's story may offend his cardiologist and continued to attempt to redirect Joseph. Dani knew that Joseph had never been in the Korean War, let alone a foxhole, but redirecting Joseph was not working so she decided to take a different approach and let him continue to repeat his story since her efforts to redirect him were not successful.

If your loved one is diagnosed with Alzheimer's or dementia, as caregivers we have little to no control over factors such as the progression or timeline of the disease. This is something that may be difficult to accept, but once we do, we can focus on the situations that we do have the ability to control to positively impact the life of our elderly loved ones.

When your loved one is in an assisted living or skilled nursing facility, there are many things over which you will not have control. Relinquishing control to a facility can relieve a caregiver's stress but at the same time create conflict over no longer having total control of the care of your loved one. As caregivers, we need to recognize the difference between what we can and cannot change and allow that recognition to permit us to move forward, focusing on positive aspects in our lives, and the things over which we do have control.

8. GIVE YOURSELF PERMISSION TO SAY NO

As a parent, the last word your children usually want to hear from you when asking for something is "No." This may be the same if you were to say it to your spouse, your boss, your parent or friend, or to a charity organization. While caution should be taken when thinking about saying no to your boss when it comes to your work performance, you can give yourself permission to say no to many other people when they ask for your time and effort and you have had the chance to weigh the pro's and cons of the situation and the extent of the potential commitment.

Learning to say "no" may begin with:

- Gathering all the information related to the extent of the commitment. As mentioned previously, it is often helpful to get it in writing, even if it is only to confirm what has been provided to you verbally. This will assist in visualizing the extent of the commitment in writing as well as confirming the details with the individual who provided them verbally.
- Developing a timeline for all other current commitments that would be concurrent with the one you may be considering.
- Prioritizing your current commitments to determine where this potential commitment may fall on your priority scale.
- Reviewing the extent of the commitment three times prior to making your decision. Split-second decision making does not allow you to make a fully informed decision. If possible, take a few days to allow yourself to process the information prior to making the final determination.
- Determining the purpose of the commitment. A friend conveyed that she volunteered for a school organization in an effort to spend more time with her children. What she found was that the commitment took her away from her children and she was sacrificing her quality family time by volunteering too much, which defeated the purpose of her reason for volunteering to begin with. Deciding the purpose of the commitment is also helpful in making your final determination of when to say no.

If you have reviewed the above steps and decide that you are going to say no but you are someone who has trouble saying no, you can do so by thanking the individual for the opportunity but explaining firmly, yet politely, that you are unable to meet the expectations of the commitment at this time.

9. FIND YOUR VOICE

Whether you have always been outspoken or more of a quiet person, now is the time to be able to effectively and efficiently use your voice. We talked about advocating for your loved one in Chapter 7, and while this is important as a caregiver, it is also important that you are able to advocate for yourself. This may be the most important time in your life to advocate for yourself, your elderly loved one, your children, and other family members for whom you are providing care and support.

As authors of this book and rehabilitation counselors, we are trained to coordinate medical and rehabilitation services, share options for services with our clients, and provide a voice for our clients when they may not be able to do so themselves. As such, we encourage you to find your voice, to ask questions and ask for help, as well as advocating for yourself and your loved one.

10. DON'T SWEAT THE SMALL STUFF!

It is always easier said than done, but we can stop focusing on the little things that we may have focused on in the past and put things into perspective. One elderly caregiver said she was embarrassed to take her spouse to church any longer as he regularly fell asleep and she didn't want others to see him asleep during the church service. A friend mentioned to her that she had seen a number of individuals fall asleep in church, or even in professional settings such as business meetings, and that not all of them were elderly, and the friend encouraged her not to focus on worrying about this possibility.

Related to children, many of us may obsess about their clothes or hair being perfect before they leave for school every day. When you are part of the Sandwich generation, caring for both your elderly loved ones and your children, sometimes something has to give. An example of this may be allowing your "tween" daughter to pick out her clothes daily from among a list of "preapproved" items. This is one way of allowing her to become independent, allowing you to focus on something else, and avoiding the early morning disagreements about what she wants to wear.

If your elderly loved one prefers to wear comfortable but less fashionable shoes than what you would like, go with it as long as he or she is safe and comfortable. Sometimes the items that we focus on are "small stuff" that we can often put into perspective so we can focus on higher priorities.

As we close this final chapter, we thank you for spending time with us through the pages of this book. We hope that the information provided will assist you in your role of providing eldercare as part of the Sandwich generation. Everyone's experience caring for children and parents differs, but we hope you have learned ways to look at your situation in a proactive manner while implementing some of the suggestions we have provided. Remember to use your resources and support systems to make this time less stressful for you and your family.

Eldercare Safety Checklist

The following Eldercare Safety Checklist provides a framework for assessing your elderly loved one's residence for potential safety hazards. The second column in the checklist enables you to identify steps that need to be taken to rectify any safety hazards.

LOCATION	FOLLOW UP NEEDED
Outside Area of Residence	
☐ Proper lighting	_____
☐ Street address visible and well lit	_____
☐ Emergency key lock box	_____
☐ Steps clear and well lit	_____
☐ Path or walkway to home clear of planters or hanging branches	_____
☐ Hand rails on steps	_____
Door/Entry Ways	
☐ Free of throw rugs	_____
☐ Free of shoes or other objects on floor	_____
☐ Well lit	_____
☐ Alarm/bell on doors (warns of wandering)	_____
Living Area	
☐ Free of throw rugs	_____
☐ Remove floor level items such as footstools, ottomans, baskets, planters, etc.	_____
☐ Non-slip flooring	_____

(continued)

(continued)

LOCATION	FOLLOW UP NEEDED
☐ Remove clutter	_____
☐ Keep pets from getting "underfoot"	_____
☐ Store pet food dishes under a table or counter top	_____
☐ Remove protruding furniture from walking areas	_____
☐ Adequate lighting throughout living area	_____
☐ Eliminate electrical cords that may be a fall hazard and use a surge protector to avoid overloading outlets	_____
☐ Properly installed smoke and carbon monoxide detectors checked regularly	_____
☐ Remove space heaters	_____

Kitchen

☐ Check refrigerator to prevent water leaking onto floor from ice or water dispenser	_____
☐ Place dishes and utensils at a level easy to reach	_____
☐ Replace dishes with plastic or nonbreakable dishes or disposable plates	_____
☐ Phone with numbers programmed for emergency contacts or a list of numbers on paper	_____
☐ Proper lighting, especially over stove	_____
☐ Kitchen fire extinguisher	_____
☐ Stove safety knobs (if needed)	_____
☐ Use electric stove top if possible to decrease potential of clothes catching fire	_____
☐ Remove mail, newspapers, or any other potentially flammable item in area of stove top	_____
☐ Remove throw rugs and items at floor level	_____
☐ Nonskid floor	_____
☐ Set temperature on water heater below 120 degrees	_____

(continued)

(continued)

LOCATION	FOLLOW UP NEEDED
☐ Label hot and cold faucets	_____
☐ Remove chemicals to avoid possible contact with food	_____
☐ Remove electrical connections from possible water contact	_____

Bathroom

☐ Apply nonslip strips to the tub or shower floor	_____
☐ Use nonskid mats for bath or shower entrance	_____
☐ Nonskid flooring	_____
☐ Proper lighting	_____
☐ Night light available	_____
☐ Remove locking mechanism or have interior door key readily available to unlock	_____
☐ Place toilet paper, toiletries, and towels between shoulder level to hip level	_____
☐ Ensure toilet is at appropriate height or purchase raised toilet seat if needed	_____
☐ Shower chair if needed	_____
☐ Set water temperature below 120 degrees	_____
☐ Grab bars by tub/toilet	_____

Bedroom

☐ Night light	_____
☐ Flashlight by bed	_____
☐ Phone by bed, with numbers programed for emergency contacts or a list of numbers on paper	_____
☐ Chair available for dressing	_____
☐ Remove items on floor	_____
☐ Audio/video monitor	_____

(continued)

(continued)

LOCATION	FOLLOW UP NEEDED
☐ Bed alarm (If appropriate)	_____
Hallways	_____
☐ Proper lighting	_____
☐ Night lights	_____
☐ Remove clutter	_____
☐ Remove objects on floor	_____
Utility/Laundry Area	_____
☐ Place detergent at reachable level	_____
☐ Remove items at floor level	_____
☐ Nonskid flooring	_____
☐ Ensure chemicals are stored safely (do not store bleach near ammonia, etc.)	_____
Medications	_____
☐ Store medicine in a secure location if your loved one is not able to oversee this process safely	_____

Caregiver Kit

As a caregiver, it is important to be prepared for all sorts of situations, from an emergency to a minor inconvenience. One way to be prepared is to create a "Caregiver Kit" that you can keep on hand so you are ready for situations that may arise. There are different items needed for a kit based on the need and type of emergency. The kit below is not all inclusive, but provides a global approach to an emergency kit. Your kit should be unique to your needs and the needs of your elderly loved one, but items that are often found in a caregiver kit include the following:

- Antibacterial wipes or soap
- Batteries
- Cash
- Cell phone and charger
- Change of clothes for loved one
- Contact lenses or eyeglasses (if appropriate)
- Diabetic supplies (if appropriate)
- Dentures (if appropriate and if spare ones are available)
- Emergency contact numbers including 911, poison control, and physician/dentist information
- Epi-Pen (If appropriate)
- Extra medication
- Flashlight
- Insurance information/medical card
- List of loved one's medication and dosages
- Manual can opener
- Nutritional supplement drinks
- Over-the-counter pain reliever (ibuprofen, acetaminophen, etc.)
- Overnight supplies for caregiver (clothes, toothbrush, comb, medications)
- Phone numbers for back-up caregiver support in the event you become ill
- Protein bars, bottled water, peanut butter, tuna fish, canned foods, and so forth, that can sustain you in an emergency

- Sanitary pads or adult undergarments (if applicable)
- Sweater or jacket for loved one
- Tissues
- Whistle

   Check with your doctor or pharmacist about the storage of medication including diabetic supplies and Epi-pens. You should replenish any supplies you use as soon as possible, and review and restock any expired supplies on a monthly basis.

Glossary

Acetylcholine   Most commonly found neurotransmitter in the peripheral and central nervous systems. In the peripheral nervous system acetylcholine aids skeletal muscle movement, as well as smooth and cardiac muscle, whereas acetylcholine in the central nervous system aids learning, memory, and mood.

Activities of Daily Living (ADL)   The tasks we do normally in daily living to care for ourselves. The ability or inability to execute ADL is also a measure of ability versus disability in many disorders.

Aggression   Hostile or destructive behavior that uses forceful action, especially when caused by frustration.

Alzheimer's disease   A degenerative brain disease that usually starts in late middle age or in old age, resulting in progressive memory loss, disorientation, changes in mood and personality, and is the most common form of dementia.

Anxiety   To have a fearful or apprehensive state of mind over an anticipated event.

Assisted Living   A housing system with limited care designed for elderly persons who need some help with ADL, but do not need to be placed in a nursing home.

Automated External Defibrillator (AED)   A small device that can automatically recognize an irregular heart beat and can then respond with an electrical shock to restore normal heart rhythm.

Baby Boomer   The name given to the increased number of babies that were born following soldiers returning home from World War II and between 1946 and 1964.

Caregiver Burnout   An emotional or physical exhaustion brought on by a long period of distress from the responsibilities of caregiving for someone. Emotional exhaustion leads to burnout much more frequently than physical exhaustion.

Caregiver Stress Syndrome   Resulting from chronic stress of ongoing caregiving tasks, caregivers experience physiological, psychological, and emotional symptoms from the strain of attending to all of the needs of a dependent loved one.

Cholinesterase Inhibitors   Used in the treatment of mild to moderate dementia due to Alzheimer's disease, this group of drugs is used to help the deficient neurotransmitter acetylcholine in the brain.

Combativeness A readiness or inclination to fight; belligerent or argumentative.

Companion Care Care provided to elderly, disabled, or those recovering from injury in which the companion performs several duties including, but not limited to, homecare, personal care, and business-related work. Also referred to as personal and home care aides.

Compensating Behaviors A psychological defense mechanism that hides your undesirable shortcomings by exaggerating desirable behaviors.

Dementia A nonreversible loss of brain function that affects memory, cognition, language, judgment, and behavior. Its most common type is Alzheimer's disease.

Depression Having persistent feelings of sadness and loss of interest, may also include physical symptoms.

Developmental Disability Originates at birth or during childhood, is expected to continue indefinitely, and substantially restricts the individual's functioning in several major life activities. More specifically, a developmental disability is a severe, chronic disability that is attributable to a mental or physical impairment or a combination of mental and physical impairments, is manifested before the person attains age 22, and results in substantial functional limitations in three or more of the following areas of major life activity: self-care, receptive and expressive language, learning, mobility, self-direction, capacity for independent living, and economic self-sufficiency.

Dietician A health professional with specialized training in diet and nutrition.

Disoriented Confused as to time, place, or personal self.

Eldercare Plan A plan that assists individuals and their loved ones in clarifying decisions about future medical treatment. This involves conversations over time about an individual's current state of health, goals, values, and preferences as well as a written document clearly stating the individual's wishes and preferences if he or she is unable to make decisions for him- or herself.

Elimination Period Length of time between when an injury or illness begins and receiving benefits from an insurer; it is often known as a waiting period.

Employee Assistance Program When a corporation provides its employees with a variety of support programs, usually aimed toward work-related difficulties, but also providing assistance when employees have problems outside of work that also can impact job performance.

Estate Total amount of assets a person possesses and/or is beneficially entitled to.

Executor   An appointed individual whose main duty is to carry out the wishes of the deceased and administer the estate of the deceased.

Geriatrics   The branch of medicine that deals with the diagnosis, treatment of diseases, and problems specific to old age.

Guardian   A person who oversees the care and/or property of another person.

Hospice Care   Supportive care given in the final phase of a terminal illness to provide comfort and quality of life with as little pain as possible, recognizing that there is no cure.

In-Home Care   A form of health service provided in the home.

Incontinence   Lacking voluntary control of excretory functions.

Long-Term Care   Care provided for individuals age 65 or above or those with a chronic or disabling condition in which constant supervision is needed.

Lucid   Completely intelligible or sane.

Magnetic Resonance Imagery (MRI)   Uses magnetic forces and radio waves in order to generate signals from the body; these signals are then used to show images of the internal body.

Medicaid Spend Down   A type of deductible on Medicaid coverage. Requires evaluation of income and assets to determine monthly deductible.

Osteomyelitis   A bacterial infection of bone and bone marrow in which the resulting inflammation can lead to a reduction of blood supply to the bone.

Palliative Care   Specialized medical care concentrated on relieving suffering of patients with both chronic and curable conditions.

Picture Board Communication Device   An electronic, touch-screen device that produces a voice output for items selected by the user.

Polypharmacy   Usage of multiple medications (simultaneously) as treatment for a single condition.

Redirecting   Channeling into a new direction; changing course or focus.

Residuary Estate   Property that remains in a deceased person's estate after all other specific gifts are made and costs are paid.

Respite Care   Short-term care of a sick person to provide relief to a regular caregiver.

Reverse Mortgage   Equity release loan to homeowners age 62 and up, allowing one to borrow money against the value of the home with no payment due until home sells or owner dies.

Sandwich Generation   A generation of people who give care to their children and their parents at the same time.

Seasonal Affective Disorder   Depressive state associated with late autumn and winter, thought to be caused by lack of sunlight.

Sensory Disability   Impairments that affect vision or hearing (among other senses).

Skilled Nursing Facility Accredited institution that serves as a long-term care facility for chronically ill and elderly.

Sundowner's Syndrome A form of symptoms much like Alzheimer's disease/dementia that become worse around late afternoon or early evening as the sun sets.

Telecommuting Using forms of telecommunication to work outside the traditional office or workplace, usually at home or in a mobile situation. Use of equipment like fax machines, phones, and computers to work from home and communicate with the workplace.

Transient Ischemic Attack (TIA) Similar to a stroke in terms of symptoms, but only lasts for a few minutes and has fewer long-term effects—a "mini-stroke."

Trustee Individual, corporation, or member of a board given the power to administer affairs and/or hold the title to property for the benefit of another person.

Wandering Aimless, not keeping a rational or sensible course.

Eldercare Experts:
Who They Are,
What They Do,
How to Find Them

- Elder law attorneys
- Eldercare financial planner
- Eldercare financial consultant
- Geriatric care manager
- Geriatric specialist
- Medicaid planner
- Senior real estate specialist

ELDER LAW ATTORNEYS

An elder law attorney is an expert in legal matters specific to older individuals as well as the applicable laws in the state in which the loved one resides. Elder law attorneys provide legal services to older persons focusing on estate planning, Medicaid, Medicare, Social Security, and veteran's benefits.

To find an elder law attorney visit:

The National Elder Law Foundation (NELF)

www.nelf.org

The only national organization certifying practitioners of elder and special needs law. NELF offers a Certified Elder Law Attorney (CELA) designation that is certified by the American Bar Association. There are more than 400 CELAs in 48 states, and their ranks are expanding steadily. Visit their website to find an eldercare attorney in your area.

The National Academy of Elder Law Attorneys, Inc. (NAELA)

www.naela.org

Founded in 1987 as a professional association of attorneys who are dedicated to improving the quality of legal services provided to seniors and people with special needs. NAELA membership is composed of practicing attorneys, judges, law professors, law students, and helping professionals in the private and public sectors who assist their clients with public benefits, probate and estate planning, guardianship/conservatorship, and health and long-term care planning, among other important issues. Visit their website to find an NAELA member attorney.

ELDERCARE FINANCIAL PLANNER

An eldercare financial planner will help your family develop a long-term financial plan to maintain independence, maximize public assistance, make financial resources last longer, and preserve resources. The cost to develop a plan varies widely, and a professional plan put together by a certified financial advisor can cost several thousand dollars. Monthly subscription services are available for around $25 per month, which provide email and phone access to certified financial professionals for questions, but they do not develop a comprehensive plan.

To find an eldercare financial planner, visit:

Certified Financial Planning Board of Standards

http://www.cfp.net

The Financial Planning Association

http://www.fpanet.org

National Association of Professional Financial Advisors

http://www.napfa.org

Eldercare Financial Consultant

An eldercare financial consultant has the same qualifications as an eldercare financial planner but does not develop a financial plan for the family. Rather, they educate the family on how to develop a plan for themselves. A typical consultation lasts up to 2 hours and costs in the area of $300.

See the resources for an eldercare financial planner, above.

GERIATRIC CARE MANAGER (GCM)

A geriatric care manager is a professional case manager, usually a licensed social worker, who assesses an elder's ability to live independently in a home environment, develops an appropriate care plan for services and equipment, and organizes needed home care services.

To find a GCM visit:

National Association of Professional Geriatric Care Managers (NAPGCM)

www.caremanager.org

GERIATRIC SPECIALIST

Physicians who often treat individuals 75 years of age and older and are familiar not only with the medical diagnoses most common to the elderly, but also the social and emotional issues that are common when working with this population.

To find a geriatric specialist contact your local hospital or health care system or visit:

The American Geriatrics Society

www.americangeriatrics.org

The AGS Foundation for Health in Aging

www.foundation.americangeriatrics.org

MEDICAID PLANNER

According to Payingforseniorcare.com, Medicaid planners help clients structure their financial resources and prepare documentation to ensure the best possibility of being accepted into the Medicaid program. They create trusts, manage asset transfers, and convert countable assets into exempt assets to ensure eligibility and preserve a family's resources. In addition, they manage finances to ensure a healthy spouse has adequate income and resources to continue living independently during and after the time when his or her partner is receiving care assistance.

Medicaid planners are available through public assistance for those who meet the qualifications for free assistance. Private Medicaid planners are also available for hire.

SENIOR REAL ESTATE SPECIALIST (SRES)

Senior real estate specialists are certified real estate agents qualified to address the needs of home buyers and sellers age 50 and above.

To find a senior real estate specialist, visit:

National Association of Realtors

www.seniorsrealestate.com

Eldercare Resources A–Z

Making the right choices regarding your elderly loved one's care is complicated at best and overwhelming at times, but knowing what resources to access can aid you greatly in decision making. The responsibility of making important life decisions with or on behalf of your parent or grandparent is less imposing when you are armed with accurate information and knowledge about agencies and organizations that can help you and your family navigate the eldercare process.

These resources are not all-inclusive, so it is important to develop effective research skills that enable you to find specific resources and assistance that meet your particular needs. Many resources vary from state to state, county to county, and locality to locality. An agency in one part of the country might be very different from an agency in another part of the country, and laws governing eldercare and estate planning vary from state to state. All of this requires a methodical and systematic approach to identifying resources that can assist you and your family in providing the best eldercare possible for your loved one.

We recommend that you contact your local Chamber of Commerce or Better Business Bureau when considering a particular agency, business, or individual to provide assistance to you and your family.

AARP

www.aarp.org

A nonprofit, nonpartisan organization that helps people 50 and over improve the quality of their lives and provides abundant resources regarding eldercare.

Administration on Aging (AoA)

www.aoa.gov

Provides senior citizens, their caregivers, and helping professionals with resources that connect visitors with federal, national, state, and local programs to assist the elderly.

AgingCare.com

www.agingcare.com
An online community that connects people caring for elderly parents to other caregivers, personalized information, and local resources.

AgingParents.com

www.agingparents.com
Information and advice for caregivers of aging parents.

Alzheimer's Association

www.alz.org
The Alzheimer's Association is the leading global voluntary health organization in Alzheimer's care and support, and the largest private, nonprofit funder of Alzheimer's research. Their website provides a 24/7 helpline, a local chapter finder, and an education and resource center.

American Automobile Association (AAA)

www.aaa.com
For information on issues related to senior driving.

The American Cancer Society

www.cancer.org
The American Cancer Society is a nationwide, community-based voluntary health organization dedicated to eliminating cancer as a major health problem.

The American Geriatrics Society (AGS)

www.americangeriatrics.org
To assist in identifying a health care professional for older adults.

The American Geriatrics Society (AGS) Foundation for Health in Aging

www.foundation.americangeriatrics.org
A nonprofit organization that provides a referral service online for geriatric specialists.

American Senior Benefits Association (ASBA)

www.asba,org

ASBA is a not-for-profit organization focused on advocacy and education for men and women age 50 and over.

American Society on Aging (ASA)

www.asaging.org

Developing leadership, knowledge, and skills to address the challenges and opportunities of a diverse aging society.

ARCH National Respite Network and Resource Center

http://archrespite.org

To help families locate respite and crisis care services in their communities.

Assisted Living Today

http://assistedlivingtoday.com

A source of information on a variety of topics related to senior living, including a comprehensive directory of both assisted living and alternative care type facilities all over the United States.

Association for Driving Rehabilitation Specialists

www.driver-ed.org

Find a certified driver rehabilitation specialist near you.

BenefitsCheckUp.Org

www.benefitscheckup.org

A free service of the National Council on Aging (NCOA), a non-profit service and advocacy organization in Washington, DC, to help identify federal, state, and private benefits programs that could save you money and cover the costs of everyday expenses.

CareLike.com

www.carelike.com

Senior living and housing information.

Caring Connections

www.caringinfo.org
Created by the National Hospice and Palliative Care Organization to provide information to caregivers related to end-of-life issues.

Centers for Medicare and Medicaid Services (CMS)

www.cms.gov
The newly named federal agency, formerly the Health Care Financing Administration, that administers the Medicare, Medicaid, and Child Health Insurance programs.

Eldercare Locator

www.eldercare.gov
A public service of the U.S. Administration on Aging that connects to services for older adults and their families.

Elder Law Answers

www.elderlawanswers.com
News and explanations of Medicaid coverage of long-term care, Medicare benefits, estate planning, guardianship, and other legal issues affecting seniors and access to a nationwide network of pre-screened attorneys who focus their practices on helping the elderly.

Family Caregiver Alliance (FCA)

www.caregiver.org
A public voice for caregivers, the FCA brings information, education, services, research, and advocacy together in one place online.

Federal Trade Commission (FTC)

www.ftc.gov
U.S. government organization to prevent business practices that are anticompetitive, deceptive, or unfair to consumers.

Full Circle America

www.fullcircleamerica.com
A virtual assisted living provider, using videoconferencing, Internet access, and web-based home monitoring to provide services to elderly persons living independently in their homes.

Gay and Lesbian Medical Association (GLMA)

www.glma.org
GLMA's mission is to ensure equality in health care for lesbian, gay, bisexual, transgender, and queer (LGBTQ) individuals and health care providers.

Human Rights Campaign

www.hrc.org
The Human Rights Campaign is America's largest civil rights organization working to achieve lesbian, gay, bisexual transgender, and queer equality.

Lambda Legal

www.lambdalegal.org
Founded in 1973, Lambda Legal is the oldest and largest national legal organization whose mission is to achieve full recognition of the civil rights of lesbians, gay men, bisexuals, transgender people, and those with HIV through impact litigation, education and public policy work.

The Lewy Body Dementia Association (LBDA)

www.lbda.org
LBDA is a nonprofit organization dedicated to raising awareness of the Lewy body dementia (LBD), supporting people with LBD and their families and caregivers, and promoting scientific advances.

Meals on Wheels Association of America (MOWAA)

www.mowaa.org
A community based senior nutrition program that is available in all 50 states and the U.S. territories.

Medicaid

www.medicaid.gov
   The official U.S. government site for information on Medicaid.

Medicare

www.medicare.gov
   The official U.S. government site for information on Medicare, including a searchable database by drug to determine eligibility for the drug manufacturer's pharmaceutical assistance programs.

National Clearinghouse for Long-Term Care Information

http://longtermcare.gov
   Developed by The U.S. Department of Health and Human Services to provide information and resources to help you and your family plan for future long-term care (LTC) needs with information on what long-term care is, how and where you can get information and services you need—now or in the future—and how to pay for services.

The National Committee for the Prevention of Elder Abuse (NCPEA)

www.preventelderabuse.org
   Dedicated to the prevention of abuse and neglect of older persons and adults with disabilities.

National Council on Aging (NCOA)

www.ncoa.org
   A nonprofit service and advocacy organization that works to help seniors find jobs and benefits, improve their health, live independently, and remain active in their communities.

The National Hospice and Palliative Care Organization (NHPCO)

www.nhpco.org
   The largest nonprofit membership organization representing hospice and palliative care programs and professionals in the United States. The organization is committed to improving end-of-life care

and expanding access to hospice care with the goal of profoundly enhancing quality of life for people dying in America and their loved ones. Includes a searchable database for local hospice or palliative care programs.

National Long-term Care Ombudsman Resource Center

www.ltcombudsman.org
   Locate an ombudsman, state agencies, and citizen advocacy groups.

National Resource Center on LGBT and Aging (A Project of SAGE)

www.lgbtagingcenter.org
   The National Resource Center on LGBT and Aging is the country's first and only technical assistance resource center aimed at improving the quality of services and support offered to lesbian, gay, bisexual, and transgender (LGBT) older adults.

National Transit Hotline

1-800-527-8279
   For information about local transit providers who receive federal funds to provide transportation to the elderly and people with disabilities.

Patient Assistance Programs—Prescription Drugs for the Uninsured

www.patientassistance.com
   A database of over 1,000 patient assistance programs designed to help those in need.

Paying for Senior Care

www.payingforseniorcare.com
   Tools and information on financial assistance, long-term care costs, finding affordable care, and understanding Medicare, Medicaid, and Veteran's benefits.

Respite Care

Assistance with paying for respite care can be found at many sources including www.caregiver.org or www.alz.org.

SAGE

www.sageusa.org
   SAGE is the world's oldest and largest nonprofit agency dedicated to serving lesbian, gay, bisexual, and transgender older people.

Seniors Real Estate Specialists™ (SRES™)

www.seniorsrealestate.com
   A website provided by the National Association of Realtors that can be used to locate a senior real estate specialist near you.

Social Security

www.socialsecurity.gov
   The official U.S. government site for information on Social Security.

The U.S. Department of Housing and Urban Development (HUD)

http://portal.hud.gov/hudportal/HUD
   Offers HUD-approved housing counselors to provide assistance to determine housing options for seniors, including information on reverse mortgages, federal housing programs, assisted living options, rural housing loans, finding in-home help, meals on wheels, and much more.

The U.S. Department of Veterans Affairs

www.va.gov
   Provides information on patient care and federal benefits for veterans and their dependents.

Index

About the Authors

Kimberly McCrone Wickert, MRC, CRC, is a nationally certified rehabilitation counselor who has more than 20 years of experience working with people with disabilities. She holds a bachelor's degree in speech pathology and audiology and a master's degree in rehabilitation counseling. Ms. Wickert has more than two decades of management and supervisory experience in a variety of professional settings. She has worked with many client populations including disabled military veterans; injured workers; and individuals with traumatic brain injuries, developmental disabilities, speech and hearing impairments, visual impairments and blindness, and orthopedic disabilities. She has also worked in occupational health and industrial rehabilitation facilities. Ms. Wickert specializes in vocational services including evaluations; career counseling; job seeking skills training; and job placement, development, and retention services. She has worked with older individuals providing rehabilitation services and has volunteered with seniors in a variety of settings including skilled nursing facilities and assisted living facilities. Ms. Wickert has also served as an adjunct faculty member at Kent State University and Wright State University.

Danielle Schultz Dresden, MEd, CRC, is a nationally certified rehabilitation counselor with more than 15 years of experience working with individuals with disabilities. Ms. Dresden has a master's degree in rehabilitation counseling and a bachelor's degree in criminology. She has worked in numerous rehabilitation settings including workers' compensation and the Veterans Administration in both direct service and supervisory capacities. She has served many client populations including individuals with developmental disabilities, substance use disorders, blindness and low vision, deafness, mobility impairments, chronic pain, and mental illness. Throughout Ms. Dresden's career, her focus has been on vocational rehabilitation services to assist people with disabilities in the pursuit of gainful employment and economic self-sufficiency. These services include vocational assessments, disability management services to employers, consultation regarding on-the-job accommodations and assistive technology, job-seeking skills training, job development and placement interventions, and career maintenance services. Ms. Dresden has also worked closely with more than 200 employers to develop transitional work policies for their employees who are recovering from work-related and non-work-related injuries. She has extensive experience coordinating eldercare services for her own family members and volunteering to assist elderly individuals in their efforts to live independently.

Phillip D. Rumrill, Jr., PhD, CRC, is a professor of rehabilitation counseling and director of the Center for Disability Studies at Kent State University. He holds a bachelor's degree in psychology, a master's degree in counseling, and a doctorate in rehabilitation. Dr. Rumrill's professional work experience includes residential services for people with developmental disabilities, substance abuse counseling, vocational counseling with people with chronic illnesses, and assistive technology training for college students with disabilities. Dr. Rumrill's research interests include the career development implications of disability, chronic illness, transition services for adolescents with disabilities, workplace discrimination, and disability issues in higher education. He has authored or co-authored more than 200 professional publications, including books entitled *Employment Issues and Multiple Sclerosis* (two editions), *Research in Rehabilitation Counseling* (two editions), *New Directions in Rehabilitation Counseling, Emerging Issues in Rehabilitation Counseling, Multiple Sclerosis, and Research in Special Education* (two editions). Dr. Rumrill has received awards for his research and program development efforts from such organizations as the National TRIO Foundation, the National Association of Student Personnel Administrators, the University of Arkansas Alumni Association, and the National Council on Rehabilitation Education.